7-DAY
SUGAR *Cleanse*

7-DAY
SUGAR *Cleanse*

Beat Your Addiction with **TASTY, EASY-TO-MAKE RECIPES**
That Nourish and Help You Resist Cravings

LEISA MALONEY COCKAYNE
founder of *Make Me Sugar Free*

PAGE STREET
PUBLISHING CO.

PAGE STREET
PUBLISHING CO.

First published in 2021 by
Page Street Publishing Co.
27 Congress Street, Suite 105
Salem, MA 01970
www.pagestreetpublishing.com

Distributed by Macmillan, sales in Canada by The Canadian Manda Group.

25 24 23 22 21   1 2 3 4 5

ISBN-13: 978-1-64567-334-7
ISBN-10: 1-64567-334-0

Library of Congress Control Number: 2020948807

Cover and book design by Rosie Stewart for Page Street Publishing Co.
Recipe styling by Leisa Maloney Cockayne
Photography by Mike Cockayne

Printed and bound in the United States

To Mike, for our love and for giving me a lifeline.
To Ruby, my love. And for being a lifeline.

Table of Contents

Foreword

As part of my doctoral studies, I spent a considerable amount of time investigating the quality of carbohydrates and the effects on mood and performance. I was therefore delighted to be asked to write the foreword for *7-Day Sugar Cleanse*. As an ex–sugar addict, Leisa should be commended for sharing her experience of removing excess and added sugar from her diet, so others can reap the benefits of this dietary modification.

We evolved from hunting for our food, and unlike today, we were highly active and where sugar was concerned, it was found naturally in fruit and vegetables. With the typical Westernized diet being highly processed and sugar-dense, it is so important to educate people about the implications to our health of excess sugar. Added sugar is causing major health issues including decaying teeth, weight gain, sleep and hormonal issues as well as the debilitating disease of Type 2 diabetes. It is essential that we respect our body, as it is the vehicle that will carry us from now until the end, and therefore it makes good sense to look after it, provide it with nutrients and allow organs to operate as effectively as possible.

In this book, Leisa refers to the saying "we are what we eat," a saying I also referred to in some early nutrition research I carried out as an undergraduate student. It was initially written by a French physician Atheleme Brillat-Savarin in 1826, where he stated, "Tell me what you eat, and I will tell you what you are." What he meant by this was that if you follow a healthy diet, you are likely to be a healthy person.

In this book, Leisa guides the reader through the transition to a healthier diet. She not only tries to educate the reader about the nature of different forms of sugar and the related health issues of their consumption, but also provides a fantastic range of attractive, simple, inspiring recipes that will provide interesting meals for breakfast, lunch and dinner without excess sugar content.

I wish Leisa, and her readers, every success with this book and its intention.

—**DR. ANNA ROBINS,** PhD in Ingestive Behavior, senior lecturer
and program leader in 'Nutrition and Exercise as Medicine'
at the University of Salford

Introduction

Hi, my name is Leisa and I'm an ex-sugar addict. Chances are, if you've picked up this book, you too might be struggling with the white stuff. The great news is, following this 7-Day Sugar Cleanse will give you sugar freedom in just one week.

This cleanse isn't about never eating sugar again; it's about breaking the sugar addiction cycle, which will allow you to make sensible food choices that are not controlled by insatiable cravings. You'll be able to eat what you want, on your terms, without being under the nagging influence of your sugar addiction.

Giving up sugar is one of the single most effective dietary changes you can make. That's a bold statement, but it's a true one. We hear about all types of diets, from Paleo to Keto to low-fat-this to low-carb-that, but cutting out sugar really is one of the best things you can do for your overall health and well-being.

Eating excess sugar can lead to a whole host of negative health and wellness issues. In the short term, these include weight gain and obesity, disturbed sleep, low energy, premature aging, brain fog and poor memory. A diet of excess sugar over a prolonged period of time might lead to more serious complications, such as Type 2 diabetes, heart disease and even strokes. Since sugar is added to roughly 80 percent of processed and packaged foods, it's easier than you think to eat too much—and it also makes it very easy for so many of us to get hooked!

In this book, I'll be taking you through a 7-day program to rid your body of sugar, while providing you with tasty, easy-to-make recipes that are nourishing, filling and, most importantly, will help keep sugar cravings at bay. You'll learn where sugar hides and how to avoid it, as well as which foods to eat and which to steer clear of. I provide lots of tips and advice for dealing with any urges to eat sweet foods. There's also additional information that will help you continue to live a low- to no-sugar lifestyle beyond the 7 days.

Together, we can beat your sugar addiction and get you on the right path to a better, healthier—and less hangry!—you.

Leisa

Getting Started

SUGAR ADDICTION: WHAT IT IS, WHY IT'S BAD FOR YOU AND HOW TO BREAK IT!

WHY ARE SO MANY PEOPLE ADDICTED TO SUGAR?

First off, sugar is a highly addictive substance. When we eat anything sweet-tasting, it triggers the release of dopamine, which is also known as the happy hormone. This is the same hormone that creates addictions to nicotine, alcohol, drugs and gambling. It makes us feel good when we eat sugar, so we begin to crave that sensation.

And it's not just that sugar is an addictive substance; there's also an evolutionary biological glitch that keeps us hooked. All sugars are made up of roughly 50 percent glucose and 50 percent fructose, and fructose is one of the only foods on earth that doesn't trigger a feeling of being satisfied. In other words, we can eat and eat it to the point of feeling sick without feeling full. How many times have you sat down to relax and watch a movie with your sweet treats, having convinced yourself that "you'll only have a few"? Halfway through the pack, you're already feeling fit to burst, but on you plow. Your belly's groaning because you've eaten so much, but the craving seems to override all common sense, and so on you plunder.

You see, thousands of years ago, food was scarcer, so when humans came across a tree full of fruit or a bush full of berries, it was in our interest to eat as many as we could before they rotted, and then to store that sugar as energy to be used later. Back then, any form of sugar was seldom come by. But, unfortunately for us, it's everywhere now. Our bodies simply haven't caught up with and evolved as quickly as the food industry.

We still physically respond to sugar—fructose—as we did all those years back, because we simply haven't developed a stop button to tell us to stop eating it. For many people, it takes them feeling physically sick before they can stop. When was the last time you ate so much fish or broccoli you felt sick? It's nearly impossible to eat that much, because our body signals when we've had enough.

For the longest time, I felt so much shame around my eating habits, and I thought I must have just lacked willpower. I'd make light work of devouring a family-size chocolate bar that I fooled myself into thinking I'd only eat a square of. Or, I'd gorge on a full packet of cookies. My sugar-free journey has proven to me that it's not our lack of willpower, it's the way our bodies respond to sugar that makes it so difficult to refuse when we're gripped with cravings. Plus, the onslaught of multimillion dollar ad campaigns at every turn encourages our sugar consumption.

Sugar and sweet foods have become psychologically associated with treats. Cakes, chocolate and ice cream are all foods that we eat to make ourselves feel good, or to reward ourselves. This is the message perpetuated in most advertising that can be seen on TV, online, on billboards and in magazines. And, unlike our hunter-gatherer predecessors, we don't have to wait to happen upon a berry bush to get a fructose hit. No, we're greeted with wall-to-wall confectionery pretty much anywhere we go: from the corner store to the gas station, hardware store or supermarket. Sugar is everywhere, so it's hardly surprising that so many people are eating too much.

SO, WHAT DOES ALL THIS EXCESS SUGAR DO TO YOUR BODY, AND WHY IS IT SO BAD?

The World Health Organization (WHO) and American Heart Association recommend that women limit their intake of added sugar to 6 teaspoons (25 g) per day and that men limit theirs to 9 teaspoons (36 g) a day. In small amounts like this, sugar doesn't have a negative effect on our health. Unfortunately, it's easy to exceed this amount when you look at the average amount of sugar in our foods—and it's posing serious health risks.

The number of Americans living with Type 2 diabetes tripled between 1990 and 2010.

The 2020 Centers for Disease Control and Prevention's (CDC's) National Diabetes Statistics Report said that 1 in 10 Americans has Type 2 diabetes. And, if sugar consumption continues at its current rate, the CDC predicted that 1 in 3 Americans will have Type 2 diabetes by 2050, according to a 2010 report.

These studies reveal the true impact excess sugar has on the overall health of so many people. They also show just how easy it is to fall into the trap of eating too much of the stuff. With the help of this book, you'll be able to gain control and break free from this unhealthy addiction.

Another interesting fact about sugar is that it isn't even a food. It contains no nutrients and provides empty calories, i.e., energy without nutrition. Sugar can actually block the absorption of minerals and vitamins.

Instead of nutrition, here's what we know sugar provides:

- Energy slumps
- Mood swings
- Poor dental health and risk of gum disease
- Diabetes, hyperglycemia and hypoglycemia
- A trigger for overeating
- Weight gain
- Older-looking skin and premature aging
- Metabolic syndrome
- Increased anxiety and irritability
- Damage to the liver
- A significant or contributory cause of heart disease, atherosclerosis, depression, senility, mental illness and hypertension

THE BENEFITS OF CUTTING OUT SUGAR

By cutting excess sugar from your diet, you can expect the following benefits:

INCREASED ENERGY LEVELS—Sugar can give you a short burst of energy, or a quick pick-me-up, when it first hits your bloodstream. Unfortunately, that short benefit gets offset by the longer-term effect of the spiked blood sugar level, which will leave you feeling more tired than before you ate the sugar. Continuing to feed a sugar addiction creates unnatural spikes and lows in your blood sugar.

WEIGHT LOSS—Fructose gets stored as fat, often as visceral fat—the most dangerous type of fat—which forms around your organs. When you quit sugar, your body starts to use up these fat stores as energy instead of glucose in your blood.

BETTER SKIN AND LOOKING YOUNGER—When we eat sugar, the molecules in the bloodstream react and create enzymes that break down the collagen and elastin in our skin.

BETTER SLEEP—Blood sugar imbalance is one of the most common causes of insomnia, yet most people are unaware that this is the cause of their sleepless nights. Eating sugar late at night spikes blood sugar levels, making it hard to sleep.

STRONGER IMMUNE SYSTEM—Excess sugar lowers the ability of the body's white blood cells to kill off bacteria, weakening your immune system. A stronger immune system means you will experience fewer bugs and colds.

BETTER BREATH—Halitosis is often caused by bad bacteria breeding in the mouth. These bacteria love sugary stuff.

BETTER ORAL HEALTH—As we learned at school, sugar feeds the bacteria that causes tooth plaque, which causes cavities.

FEWER MOOD SWINGS—Overloading yourself with sugar alters the gut-brain connection, which can create anxiety, and the sugar spikes followed by sugar crashes cause mood changes. By quitting sugar, you'll be leveling out your blood sugar throughout the day, which will help to level out your moods.

REDUCED RISK OF TYPE 2 DIABETES—Type 2 diabetes is a chronic condition that affects the way that your body metabolizes sugar, specifically glucose, which is your body's energy source. Cutting sugar from your diet will significantly reduce your chances of developing Type 2 diabetes, along with all of its complications, including liver failure, potential loss of vision and even loss of limbs.

FEWER JOINT AND MUSCLE ACHES—Sugar triggers the release of inflammatory messengers, called *cytokines*, and this constant inflammation stresses the joints. Sugar also depletes the body of important minerals, some of which are required for proper muscle function and recovery.

BETTER SEX—Insulin resistance brought on by consuming excessive amounts of sugar lowers the levels of testosterone, which plays a big part in the sexual well-being of both men and women.

REDUCED STRESS ON YOUR LIVER—Pretty much all sugar is made up of 50 percent glucose and 50 percent fructose. Any cells in the body can process glucose, but only the liver can process fructose. Continually overloading the liver with fructose can lead to non-alcoholic fatty liver disease, a condition in which fat builds up in your liver.

LESS VISCERAL FAT—Excessive fructose that can't be processed by the liver can turn into visceral fat. This type of fat can release free fatty acids, increasing inflammation, as well as a protein that can increase insulin resistance. So, when you give up the sugary treats, you'll be giving your organs a breather.

A HEALTHIER HEART—Studies have shown that large quantities of sugar can damage human heart tissue and has caused heart disease in lab animals. Chronic high blood sugar levels lead to a condition called *atherosclerosis*, or hardening of the arteries. This condition is associated with heart disease and heart failure.

AN IMPROVED MEMORY—Too much sugar has a direct and detrimental effect on your memory and brain function, so much so that heavy consumption of sugar over a long period of time can actually result in permanent brain damage.

INCREASED FEELING OF HAPPINESS—Studies have shown a highly significant correlation between sugar consumption and the annual rate of depression. By cutting sugar out of your diet, you can expect your mood not only to level out, but also to lift.

WHY THIS 7-DAY SUGAR CLEANSE WILL HELP

One of the reasons you might be reaching for sugary snacks, and unconsciously putting your health and happiness at risk, is that you are trapped in a sugar-addiction cycle. If you eat a high-sugar content breakfast, you spike your blood sugar levels. To cope with the excess sugar, your body will overcompensate in its removal from your bloodstream, and, by 11 a.m., you'll likely get your first slump, caused by low blood sugar.

When your brain detects these low levels, it looks for a quick fix to bring them back up. You experience this as a craving, but it's really your body's desire for another snack to boost your blood sugar levels.

By eating high-sugar foods throughout the day, you end up on a constant roller coaster, with constantly fluctuating blood sugar levels that cause cravings and energy slumps.

With this 7-day sugar reset, you will break that cycle. By the end of the week, you will have minimized your cravings for sugar. By making the right food choices to keep your blood sugar levels stable, you will avoid spikes and slumps and prevent the onset of insatiable urges to eat sugar. Once your cravings are minimized, it'll be much easier to live a healthier, happier, lower-sugar life.

In following this cleanse program, you'll avoid triggering the sugar-addiction roller coaster, starting first thing in the morning by eating solid breakfasts that are low in sugar, low in simple carbohydrates and high in protein, fiber, complex carbs and nutrients.

The same principles apply for lunch and evening meals, too. So, we end up nourishing our bodies properly, while providing a consistent source of slow-release energy, preventing blood sugar spikes and cravings.

WHAT WILL MY LIFE BE LIKE, FREE FROM SUGAR ADDICTION?

Giving up a bad habit, such as smoking, is not really giving up anything: It's freeing yourself from an addiction. It's the same with sugar: You aren't really giving up anything. Instead, you are developing a whole new freedom in which you are no longer controlled by unnatural urges—urges that tell you what to eat and when, rather than the other way around.

When we succumb to sugar cravings, we make bad food choices that effect our whole life and well-being.

Cutting sugar from your diet is simply freeing yourself from an addiction.

UNDERSTANDING AND PREPARING FOR YOUR SUGAR CLEANSE

THE NUTRITION PRINCIPLES BEHIND YOUR 7-DAY SUGAR CLEANSE

As the age-old saying goes, "We are what we eat." And as I'm sure you already know, not all foods are made equal; so, I will tell you how the recipes in the sugar cleanse will help you beat sugar cravings.

Eating the right types of food can nourish our bodies, provide what we need to function optimally and prevent cravings. By contrast, eating the wrong foods provides very little nourishment, depletes our health and triggers the desire for more junk. By understanding a little bit about how these different foods affect our bodies, we can begin to understand the basic principles of the cleanse.

PRINCIPLE 1: AVOID SIMPLE CARBS—None of the meals in my program contain simple carbohydrates.

In a healthy diet, we get the majority of our energy from eating carbohydrates, which convert into glucose, the energy source that powers our bodies. There are two types of carbohydrates: simple, or bad, carbs and complex, or good, carbs.

Simple carbohydrates, such as white bread, pasta and pastries, are usually made from processed white flour products. However, white rice and even potatoes fall under the simple, or bad, carb category. These carbs break down rapidly and release glucose into the bloodstream very quickly, causing a blood sugar spike just like if you'd eaten something high in sugar. Simple carbs deliver their energy quickly, but in return deliver a slump equally as fast.

This cleanse will eliminate simple carbohydrates from your diet. You'll be eating only complex carbohydrates.

Complex carbohydrates are structurally more complicated and are found in whole grains, vegetables, oatmeal and brown rice. The complicated structure, along with the high fiber content that many complex carbs contain, means that the glucose is released into the bloodstream at a much lower, more controlled rate, creating a much more stable blood sugar level. These food types deliver sustained energy over a longer period of time, with no noticeable spikes or slumps. The fiber they contain is essential for our digestive and gut health.

PRINCIPLE 2: FILL UP ON PROTEIN—Protein is the other vital component to your sugar-free diet. Reducing sugars and carbs and focusing on fats and proteins can help you to feel fuller longer, due to the simple fact that protein takes a lot longer to digest than carbohydrates. Protein also suppresses the hunger hormone, called *ghrelin*. So, a high-protein diet typically leads to a natural reduction in food intake.

Good sources of protein are lean meats, fish, chicken, eggs, dairy products like cheese, milk and yogurt, as well as beans and legumes, like chickpeas and lentils. Finally, seeds and nuts are also high in protein, and will often be full of healthy fats and oils that we need. These proteins are a good alternative to meat, if you are interested in a more plant-based diet.

PRINCIPLE 3: EAT THE RIGHT FATS—Fat has been demonized over the years, and has been blamed for making people overweight. The truth about fat is very different. It can be found in most foods, and, when eaten in sensible amounts, can have numerous health benefits, including helping the body better absorb certain vitamins and minerals. Fat doesn't make you fat—as long as you eat the right type.

Despite fat being seen previously as the enemy of a healthy diet, it turns out it's more likely to be sugar that raises your cholesterol and contributes to heart disease.

In the past, it seemed obvious to choose low-fat or fat-free products when one is trying to lose weight. But the low-fat options often contain more sugar than their full-fat counterparts, making them more harmful to health. When food companies take the fat out of a product, there's a good chance it'll start to taste like cardboard. So, they pump it full of sugar to get back flavor. What you end up with is a product that is low in fat but high in sugar. Ironically, this added sugar will most likely turn into fat in your body.

Different foods provide the four types of fat: polyunsaturated, monounsaturated, saturated and trans fats. It's worth noting that, just like food, not all fats are equal.

Polyunsaturated fats are found in nuts and fish as omega-3 and omega-6 fats. They play an important part in keeping our hearts healthy.

Monounsaturated fats are also found in nuts, as well as in avocados and olive oil, and are thought to help reduce heart disease and inflammation.

Saturated fats are found in foods such as eggs, meat, butter and coconut oil, and they can contribute to our metabolic function. There is mixed opinion on saturated fat, which some consider the middle ground between healthy and bad fats.

Everyone agrees that trans fats need to be avoided at all costs. This type of fat is created via a process called *hydrogenation*, turning liquid fat into solid fat by warping it under very high heat. Trans fat raises the level of bad cholesterol and can increase the risk of heart disease. This type of fat is found in processed foods and deep-fried foods. It also lurks in cakes, crackers and even in some so-called healthy protein and breakfast bars. By cutting out these junk foods, you'll cut out the sugar and keep trans fats out of your diet.

Eating healthy fat is a very important part of our daily diets. Good fats keep you fuller for longer, keeping hunger at bay. That's good news, because, as long as we're full, we don't go looking for sweet snacks.

PRINCIPLE 4: AVOID SUGARY DRINKS—Sugary drinks can very quickly take you over your recommended daily sugar allowance. For some people, cutting out high-sugar sodas is one of the simplest dietary changes they can make. This includes diet and zero-calorie varieties—it's important to cut out all sweet triggers, even if they are coming from alternative sweeteners—in order to reset your palate. Fruit juices are also very high in sugar content: A glass of orange juice can contain as much sugar as a can of soda. For the duration of the sugar cleanse, cut out all sugary drinks and don't use sugar or sweeteners in your tea and coffee. Instead, try drinking carbonated water with a squeeze of lemon or lime, and switch to herbal teas.

THE NEXT 7 DAYS

Over the weeklong cleanse, we'll cut out sugar completely from your diet, and fill you with lots of tasty, nourishing meals and snacks based on the guidelines I outlined for you in the previous section. On page 23, you will find your 7-Day Meal Plan, filled with recipes for breakfast, lunch and evening meals. Feel free to mix and match any meals from any of the days, if you wish.

I also include a list of snacks that are designed to keep you feeling full between meals, and to give you something to nibble on if you get any cravings. Feel free to eat as many of these snacks whenever you desire—this isn't a calorie-controlled diet, it's all about healthy eating.

The meal plan has been designed to focus on nutrition and to cram in vitamins, minerals, fiber, healthy fats, proteins and complex carbs, using only whole foods. If your body is receiving all the goodness it needs, it won't be in search of quick-fix energy sources, which lead to cravings and to you reaching for the cookies.

Cutting out every type of sugar, including fruit, gives your metabolism time to reset and enables you to break the dreaded sugar-addiction cycle.

I have also included lots of tasty meal ideas designed to keep you on the straight and narrow once you've completed your cleanse. These recipes stick to the principles I outlined above, but give you more meal options as you embrace the new, healthier you.

There are also dessert recipes for post-cleanse that reintroduce sugars, in the form of fruits. These recipes are a healthier take on some of the most popular desserts, since nutrient-dense and high-fiber ingredients replace the sugar. The recipes are sweetened only with dates, apple, banana or prunes. Post-cleanse, you will notice how sweet things taste and that a little will go a long way. Instead of eating empty-calorie, sugar-drenched desserts, choose these healthy, nutritious options on special occasions.

It's worth remembering that the cleanse is not about you never eating sugar again. This cleanse is about helping you gain control over your eating habits and sugar cravings. It's good to have healthy alternatives, so you don't slip back to old habits. You'll notice it's very hard to overeat when you're eating real foods.

PREPARING FOR YOUR CLEANSE

Before you take on this 7-Day Sugar Cleanse, there are a few things that you should do in order to make life a little easier.

THE BIG CLEAR-OUT—First, you'll need to get rid of all sugary and sweet foods from your fridge and cupboards. It's amazing how loudly that packet of cookies can call you from a cupboard, if you know it's there. You can be watching TV or working away, and suddenly you remember the bar of chocolate in your cabinet. It nags and nags until you cave. Then, you're wolfing it down. This is normal, by the way. This is symptomatic of the physiological and mental effects of sugar addiction being in play. It can be very hard to resist. By ridding your home of anything sweet, you'll make things a lot easier for yourself when the sugar pangs hit. If it's not there, you can't eat it.

Quitting sugar can be difficult enough without any temptations to lead us astray, so this clear-out is crucial. Just get rid of it, and all of it. If you share a house or apartment with someone else, you could ideally get them to detox with you. Failing that, ask them to hide their treats in their own rooms. Also, politely ask them not to eat anything sweet in front of you—you need all the help you can get!

LEARN TO READ THE LABELS—Do we really know what's in our food? Learning to read your food labels is a huge revelation. What you perceive as a healthy snack may actually be loaded with sugar. The higher up in the list of ingredients you find a food type, the more it contains. If sugar is one of the first five ingredients, then that product is high in added sugar. Sugar content may also be listed under different names, to make a product appear less sugary.

There are at least 60 different types of sugar, including table sugar, brown sugar, honey, agave syrup, glucose and maple. No matter what they are called, once you eat them, they all break down in your body exactly the same. So, swapping out sugar for honey really doesn't change a thing. I've listed many of the different names for sugars on the following page.

When reading food labels, look at the sugar and added sugar data in the carbohydrates section. It will give you the number of naturally occurring grams of sugar in the product, as well as the number of grams of sugar that has been added in the processing of that food. Remember, the WHO daily guidelines are 6 teaspoons (25 g) for a woman and 9 teaspoons (36 g) for a man, so always check food labels to see how much sugar you might be eating. You'd be surprised just how much sugar there is in some of the most innocent-looking products.

SHOP FOR THE WEEK TO SAVE YOURSELF FROM TEMPTATION!—The food industry is a very powerful entity that uses well-researched psychology and stealth-marketing strategies to persuade us to buy what we don't really want or need. Then, there are the supermarkets, which are cleverly designed to lead us through the aisles in a very specific way, with items stacked on shelves deliberately in the best way to tempt us to purchase. And, it's not just the supermarkets. At most types of stores, we are bombarded with a visual array of sweets and chocolate bars.

The supermarket is usually our first point of contact with all that is bad for us. So, here's something to remember: If you don't put it in the basket, you can't buy it. A brief period of willpower while doing the shopping can save you a hundred temptations later at home. And, remember, whatever you do, never shop when you are hungry!

Of course, the best way to avoid any of these temptations is simply to stay away: Shop less, shop online or get someone else to do it. If that's not possible, make a shopping list and stick to it.

WATCH OUT FOR SO-CALLED HEALTHY FOODS—There is a whole industry based on people's desire to get healthy. Yet, most of the so-called healthy options are packed with added sugar. The low-fat yogurts, granola and muesli bars, juices and cereals you find in supermarkets that may look like good choices initially may have a high sugar content. Take a quick look at the labels, and you'll see just how bad for you some products really are. Remember, check labels to see how much sugar a product contains.

CONFIDE IN OTHERS—It's also worth letting family and friends know you're quitting sugar, as having that extra support and accountability can help you through any tough patches. Find an ally, someone who will be your cheerleader and encourage you. Get them to quit sugar with you!

Sneaky Names for Sugar

When you're doing your big clearout, check for the following various types of sugar added to packaged foods. If any of these products are in the first five ingredients on a food label, the product should definitely not be part of your low- or no-sugar diet.

- Agave Nectar
- Agave Syrup
- Barbados Sugar
- Barley Malt
- Beet Sugar
- Blackstrap Molasses
- Brown Rice Syrup
- Brown Sugar
- Butter Syrup
- Cane Juice Crystals
- Cane Sugar
- Caramel
- Carob Syrup
- Coconut Palm Sugar
- Confectioners' Sugar
- Corn Sweetener
- Corn Syrup
- Corn Syrup Solids
- Date Sugar
- Dehydrated Cane Juice
- Demerara Sugar
- Dextran
- Dextrose
- Diastase
- Diastatic Malt
- Ethyl Maltol
- Evaporated Cane Juice
- Free-Flowing Brown Sugar
- Fructose
- Fruit Juice
- Fruit Juice Concentrate
- Galactose
- Glucose
- Glucose Solids
- Golden Sugar
- Golden Syrup
- Grape Sugar
- HFCS
- High-Fructose Corn Syrup
- Honey
- Icing Sugar
- Invert Sugar
- Lactose
- Malt Syrup
- Mannose
- Maple Syrup
- Molasses
- Muscovado Sugar
- Organic Raw Sugar
- Panocha
- Powdered Sugar
- Raw Sugar
- Refiner's Syrup
- Saccharose
- Sorghum Syrup
- Sucrose
- Sugar
- Sweet Sorghum
- Syrup
- Treacle
- Turbinado Sugar

HOW TO SUCCESSFULLY TACKLE THE CLEANSE

It is highly likely that you are going to experience some type of sugar cravings when you first cut it from your diet. These may be mild or they may be quite strong, depending on the previous quantity of sugar in your diet. By keeping your body full and well-nourished with the meals in this book, you will already be making great steps to fend these off.

Sugar cravings are a transient sensation—they can come and go—and it's up to us not to roll over and give in. We are all capable of defeating these urges. Once you do it, you'll find that the sensation of joy and well-being in knowing you are getting stronger and able to make your own food choices far outweighs the fleeting experience of succumbing to sugar. We all have the power to stop eating junk; we just need to get into the right mindset. If you do experience cravings, here are some of my tips to deal with them.

NEVER ALLOW YOURSELF TO BECOME HUNGRY—Make sure you eat three good meals per day with snacks between. Never skip meals, such as breakfast. The hungrier we get, the easier it is for our resolve to be broken. Hunger itself creates low blood sugar levels, which leads to cravings, so make sure that you keep plenty of savory snacks at hand.

The meals in my cleanse plan are specifically designed to keep you feeling full as well as provide the nutrition your body needs to avoid triggering cravings.

LEARN THE DIFFERENCE BETWEEN HUNGER AND A CRAVING—We eat when we are hungry, and we eat when we crave something, but we do both for completely different reasons. Hunger is our body's natural trigger for food as an energy source.

Unfortunately, with sugar, the more you eat, the more you will end up craving. Once our blood sugar levels drop, we crave another sugar hit to bring them back up again. Become familiar with the two different feelings. Do you actually feel hungry, or are you hankering after something to satiate a craving? When you really focus on it, the two feelings are very different. The more you learn to really tune in to your body's signals, the more you will recognize hunger as opposed to cravings.

DRINK PLENTY OF WATER—This is something we hear all the time, yet it is the very thing we need reminding of the most. It's surprisingly easy for us to mistake thirst for hunger, so make sure you keep yourself well-hydrated. Drinking plenty of water between meals will create an additional sensation of fullness.

AVOID TRIGGERS—Think about your normal weekly routine, and try to figure out where you might be triggered into eating sugary foods. Maybe you meet a friend for coffee once a week and always end up having a slice of cake or a cookie, as well. Perhaps you eat out in a favorite restaurant and always have dessert. It's a good idea to avoid these places while you do your 7-Day Sugar Cleanse, to prevent any slipups. Also, be mindful of your weak times, that time of day when the first slump is likely to hit, or post-dinner, when you crave something tasty. If you know these are your temptation soft spots, change up your routine. At the time of your first slump, go stand outside for some fresh air. If after dinner is a weak time, call someone or clear your dishes and clean up right away, so that you're distracted.

GIVE IT FIVE—As a last resort, if you do experience very strong cravings, just tell yourself you'll have something sweet in five minutes. Hold out for those five minutes and then repeat the process. Before you know it, you'll have become distracted by something else or the craving will have subsided.

SO, CAN LIFE EVER BE SWEET AGAIN?

Yes, it can! For one, your life will immediately become sweeter by freeing yourself from an addiction. Once you have broken free of your sugar-addiction cycle, you will notice that smaller amounts of sugar will taste sweeter to you. You'll notice just how sickly-sweet processed foods taste. This 7-day cleanse process will quite literally reset your palate. As a result, naturally sweet-tasting foods will taste better than you can imagine, and you will find that a little sugar goes a long way. The biggest thing for me was the taste of a lemon—after I gave up processed sugar, it was transformed from bitter and sour to punchy and refreshing. You'll have the wonderful opportunity to taste things all over again.

The idea of this reset is to do just that—reset your system and give it a reboot. By readjusting your palate, you simply won't need as much sweetener of any kind in order to get the same taste. When you eliminate processed and refined sugar from your diet, you give every cell in the body a chance to reset.

At the end of this 7-day cleanse, you will have awakened your taste buds and physical cravings will be curbed, enabling you to simply enjoy the occasional sweet treat as exactly that—occasional. I've said it a few times already: When you stop eating sugar, you stop craving it.

Having gained control over your body's addiction, you will naturally eat a more healthy and balanced diet, because you—not your cravings—will be deciding what and when to eat. You won't be a slave to cravings that force you to make bad food decisions. You will feel healthier all around.

And, remember, you are not giving up anything; you are freeing yourself. You are simply gaining your freedom and a happier, healthier, more energized you!

The 7-Day Sugar Cleanse

		7-DAY MEAL PLAN
DAY 1	**BREAKFAST**	Coconut and Vanilla Overnight Oats (page 27)
	LUNCH	Spicy Lentil Soup (page 43)
	DINNER	Turkey and Harissa Burgers with Lime and Cilantro Brown Rice (page 59)
DAY 2	**BREAKFAST**	Bo-ho-llandaise Poached Eggs (page 35)
	LUNCH	Quinoa and Goat Cheese Burgers (page 44)
	DINNER	Pulled Hot Sauce Chicken with Sweet Potato and Chunky Guac (page 60)
DAY 3	**BREAKFAST**	Savory Savior Pancakes (page 32)
	LUNCH	Easy, Breezy Broccoli and Pesto Soup (page 48)
	DINNER	Mozzarella Beef Meatballs and Garlic Cauli Rice (page 63)
DAY 4	**BREAKFAST**	Lebanese Spicy Eggs (page 28)
	LUNCH	Satay Chicken and Rainbow Salad (page 47)
	DINNER	Sage Pork Cutlets with Buttery Sweet Potato Mash (page 66)
DAY 5	**BREAKFAST**	Fully Fed Fry-Up (page 31)
	LUNCH	Curry Sweet Potato Cakes (page 51)
	DINNER	Parma Ham and Arugula Cauli Pizza (page 69)
DAY 6	**BREAKFAST**	Breakfast Tacos (page 36)
	LUNCH	Chickpea and Mushroom Stroganoff (page 52)
	DINNER	Tandoori Chicken and Paneer Kebabs (page 70)
DAY 7	**BREAKFAST**	Asparagus, Eggs and Dreamy Lemon Drizzle (page 39)
	LUNCH	Chili Black Bean Soup (page 55)
	DINNER	Lamb Koftas and Mint Yogurt Dip (page 73)

BREAKFAST

This 7-Day Sugar Cleanse is designed to create balance and homeostasis in the body, which will help minimize sugar cravings.

What we choose for our breakfast is profoundly important to maintaining this balance—breakfast is the meal that sets us up for the day. Eating the right types of foods first thing in the morning keeps us full and provides us with slow-release energy, which balances our blood sugar levels. In contrast, when we eat sugar-laden food first thing in the morning, we get a big spike in blood sugar, and then a crash. This blood sugar roller coaster triggers more cravings for sugar throughout the day.

Not to mention, when we eat too many foods that spike blood sugar, it puts pressure on the adrenal glands to produce *cortisol*, the stress hormone, to cope with any sugar crashes. Too much cortisol can lead to all sorts of health issues: It can interfere with weight loss, contribute to high blood pressure, disrupt digestion and trigger the blood sugar roller coaster. That is not the best way to start your day.

During this cleanse, you will avoid breakfasts that cause blood sugar to spike—such as sugary cereals, muffins, sweet yogurts and bread. You'll instead opt for a high-protein meal like Bo-ho-llandaise Poached Eggs (page 35), Breakfast Tacos (page 36) or my Fully Fed Fry-Up (page 31), which promotes satiety and will help to keep blood sugar and energy levels balanced. You should aim to eat these breakfasts within 30 minutes of waking, to ensure your blood sugar levels don't drop, as well as to stop you from getting too hungry and grabbing the first muffin or donut you see!

In addition to including protein, these breakfast recipes have been designed to include slow-release energy, using specific foods that provide antioxidants, vitamins, minerals, healthy fats and fiber.

COCONUT AND VANILLA OVERNIGHT OATS

This is one of my favorite go-to breakfasts; it always sets me up for the day. Oats are a good source of slow-release energy and are a great food for helping with anxiety. They contain the amino acid tryptophan, which converts to the happy hormone serotonin, which can help promote relaxation. The addition of chia and flax seeds makes this more filling and boosts the fiber and protein content. The addition of nuts delivers healthy, filling fats, while the spices give off the most beautiful smells, as well as a big burst of flavor. The cinnamon adds more than just a pop of taste though: It also helps to curb sugar cravings and can help blood sugar levels.

Serves 2

1⅔ cups (140 g) rolled oats, divided

3 tbsp (30 g) chia seeds, divided

3 tbsp (30 g) flaxseeds, divided

3 tbsp (30 g) mixed nuts, divided (optional)

1 tbsp (8 g) cinnamon, divided

½ tsp freshly grated nutmeg, divided

½ tsp ground ginger, divided

⅓ cup (30 g) dessicated coconut, divided (optional)

1⅔ cups (400 ml) coconut milk (or oat milk for creaminess), divided, plus more for serving

1 tbsp (15 ml) vanilla, divided

Divide the oats, chia seeds, flaxseeds, nuts, if using, cinnamon, nutmeg, ginger and coconut, if using, between two jars or big mugs. Mix the ingredients together, then pour half of the coconut milk and vanilla into each jar. Stir until the ingredients are well combined. Cover the jars and refrigerate them overnight.

For serving, stir in more coconut milk to loosen everything up. In the colder months, I love to warm up my porridge. To warm, pour the overnight oats into a saucepan and heat over medium heat for 3 minutes, or until the oats start to bubble a little.

LEBANESE SPICY EGGS

When it comes to sugar cravings, you need to give the body the nutrients it needs so it doesn't crave quick energy from the wrong foods. Luckily, the egg has earned the title "nature's multivitamin" for its nutrient profile, which includes an array of vitamins, minerals, healthy fats and high-quality protein. This Middle Eastern dish is a healthy, delicious, nutritious option and hums with flavor, heat and texture. It's all you need, in one dish!

Serves 4

FOR THE EGGS

1 tbsp (15 ml) olive oil

1 large onion, thinly sliced

4 cloves garlic, finely chopped

1 tbsp (15 g) harissa paste

1 tsp smoked paprika

½ tsp cumin

1 tsp ground coriander

2⅓ cups (400 g) drained and rinsed canned chickpeas (optional)

2 zucchinis, finely diced

1 red bell pepper, sliced

¼ cup (60 ml) vegetable stock

1 (28-oz [794-g]) can chopped tomatoes

Salt, to taste

6⅔ cups (200 g) baby spinach

4 large eggs

FOR SERVING

5 tbsp (5 g) chopped fresh cilantro

1 medium avocado, sliced

½ tsp chili flakes (more or less, depending on your heat preference)

⅓ cup (80 ml) plain full-fat Greek yogurt

2 tbsp (8 g) chopped fresh parsley

For the eggs, heat the oil in a large frying pan over medium heat, then add the onion and fry it for 5 minutes, or until it's browned. Stir in the garlic, harissa, paprika, cumin, coriander and chickpeas, if using, and fry the mixture for 2 to 3 minutes, or until the mixture starts to bubble a bit.

Add the zucchinis and red bell pepper to the pan, pour in the stock and cook the mixture for 2 to 3 minutes longer, or until the liquid starts to reduce and thicken. Then, add the tomatoes, season the mixture with the salt and cook it for 5 minutes, until the veggies are tender. Then fold in the spinach. As the spinach begins to wilt, use the back of a spoon to make four shallow holes in the mixture. Crack an egg into each hole.

Cover the pan, and cook the mixture for 2 minutes, or until the egg whites turn white and are no longer translucent; if you prefer your eggs more done, cook them longer.

For serving, top the eggs with the cilantro, avocado, chili flakes, yogurt and parsley.

FULLY FED FRY-UP

Regularly skipping breakfast fatigues the adrenals, which is bad news for our blood sugar levels and our overall health. Additionally, what we choose to eat first thing is key to successfully getting through the day sugar-free! This breakfast feast is rich in protein and fiber-filled veggies and is a powerful, filling start to the day. The best part is that the whole lot can be thrown into the same pan and left to cook away.

1 tbsp (15 g) butter

8 oz (227 g) good-quality, sugar-free sausages

4 beefsteak or large tomatoes, chopped

7 oz (200 g) mushrooms, chopped

1½ cups (140 g) fresh asparagus spears

3 oz (80 g) halloumi, sliced

10 cups (300 g) spinach

Heat the butter in a large frying pan. Add the sausages, and cook them as the package directs.

When the sausages are cooked, add the tomatoes, mushrooms and asparagus to the pan and cook them for a few minutes, until they are softened. Make room in the pan for the halloumi, and cook each side for 3 minutes, until golden brown. Add the spinach and cook it for a few seconds, or until wilted; remove the spinach from the heat before it cooks down too much.

Divide the sausages, vegetables and halloumi among four plates, and serve the fry-up.

SAVORY SAVIOR PANCAKES

When we think pancakes, they're nearly always dripping in a sweet syrup, but not these guys. These savory saviors are so called because they are a delicious, fluffy alternative that can be topped with avocado, tomato, mushroom, spinach or whatever you fancy. You can also personalize this with whatever spices get you fired up in the morning, such as cumin or chili powder instead of paprika. As well as providing you with nourishing fuel for the day, this recipe helps you reimagine your favorite breakfast by cutting out an overload of excessive sweetness.

FOR THE PANCAKES

3 large eggs

½ cup (120 g) cream cheese or ricotta

2 tbsp (15 g) buckwheat flour

Pinch of salt

Pinch of paprika (optional)

1 tbsp (4 g) chopped fresh chives

Pat of butter

OPTIONAL TOPPINGS

Sliced avocado

Chopped tomato

Sliced mushrooms

Chopped ham

Preheat the oven to 370°F (185°C, gas mark 5), and line an ovenproof plate with foil.

For the pancakes, in a food processor or blender, mix the eggs, cheese, flour, salt, paprika, if using, and chives for a couple of minutes, or until the ingredients have formed a smooth batter.

Melt the butter over medium heat in a frying pan, and cover the base of the pan with a thin layer of the batter. Cook the pancake for 2 minutes, until brown on one side, then carefully flip it over and cook the other side for 2 minutes, until golden brown. Transfer the pancake to the prepared plate, and put it in the warm oven until you're ready to serve it. Repeat the process, transferring the pancakes to the oven, until you've used up all the mixture.

For serving, plate the pancakes and, if desired, top them with the avocado, tomato, mushrooms and ham.

BO-HO-LLANDAISE POACHED EGGS

Eggs with hollandaise sauce always seem to be served with a white muffin that will trigger the blood sugar roller coaster—and your resulting cravings—for the rest of the day. So, here's a wonderfully sugar-proofed version that delivers on the flavor and still has all the best bits. The stodgy traditional muffin is swapped out for the healthy mushroom, which is loaded with greens and topped with a decadent hollandaise sauce.

Serves 4

EGGS

Pinches of salt, divided

4 large portobello mushrooms, stemmed

Pinch of pepper

1 tbsp (15 g) butter, divided

4 large eggs

2 cups (60 g) spinach or kale, sauteed or raw

Pinch of red pepper flakes (optional)

BO-HO-LLANDAISE SAUCE

¼ cup (60 g) butter

3½ tbsp (55 ml) mayonnaise

2 tbsp (30 ml) heavy cream

1 tbsp (15 g) Dijon mustard

2 tsp (10 ml) lemon juice

Pinch of salt and pepper

For the eggs, preheat the oven to 370°F (185°C, gas mark 5), and place a wire rack on a baking sheet.

Then, start boiling a saucepan of water with a pinch of the salt for the poached eggs. While you're waiting for the water to boil, season the mushrooms with another pinch of salt and a pinch of pepper, and divide the butter equally among the mushrooms. Then, place them on the prepared rack, and bake them for 15 minutes, or until the mushrooms are browned and juices are running out of them.

Once the water has reached a boil, reduce the heat until it's just simmering. Slip the eggs into the water, one at a time, and poach the eggs for 3 minutes for a soft egg or 5 minutes for a hard egg.

Make the hollandaise while the eggs are poaching. In a saucepan, combine the butter, mayonnaise, cream, mustard and lemon juice. Cook the sauce over low heat, gently stirring, for 1 minute, or until the ingredients are well combined. Cook the sauce for 3 to 4 minutes, or until just before it starts to bubble, continuing to stir gently to keep the sauce smooth in consistency. Remove the sauce from the heat.

Remove the mushrooms from the oven, and top them with the spinach. Using a slotted spoon, place the poached eggs on the mushrooms, then top them with the sauce. Sprinkle the sauce with the salt and pepper and red pepper flakes, if desired, and serve.

BREAKFAST TACOS

This recipe has a great balance of healthy fats, fiber, vitamins and minerals. It's a great one to help regulate blood sugar levels and bolster the immune system, which can be weakened by excessive sugar consumption. The cilantro helps trigger the digestive enzymes. Health benefits aside, this tastes divine!

Serves 4

TORTILLAS

1 cup (100 g) finely ground almond flour

⅓ cup (37 g) coconut flour

1 tsp baking powder

1 tsp xanthan gum

1 large egg

½ tsp salt

2 tbsp (30 ml) lukewarm water, plus more if needed

1 tbsp (15 ml) olive oil

SALSA

2 beefsteak tomatoes, chopped

1 small red onion, finely chopped

1 clove garlic, minced

1 chile, seeded and finely chopped (optional)

1¾ cups (28 g) finely chopped fresh cilantro

Juice of 1 lime

1 tsp salt

FILLING

⅔ cup (110 g) drained and rinsed canned black beans

¾ cup (80 g) grated Gruyère or Cheddar cheese

1 avocado, sliced

1 tbsp (7 g) smoked paprika

Pinch of salt and pepper

¼ cup (60 ml) crème fraîche or sour cream (optional)

For the tortillas, preheat the oven to 350°F (175°C, gas mark 4), and cut eight 6-inch (15-cm) squares of parchment paper.

Mix the almond flour, coconut flour, baking powder, xanthan gum, egg and salt in a food processor or a blender for a few seconds, until the ingredients are combined. Slowly add the water, a teaspoon at a time, pulsing after each addition, until the dough clumps together and forms a ball in the processor.

Remove the dough from the processor, shape it into a ball and wrap it in plastic wrap. Let the dough rest in the refrigerator for 10 minutes.

Make the salsa while the dough rests. In a large bowl, combine the tomatoes, onion, garlic, chile, if using, cilantro, lime juice and salt.

Remove the dough from the fridge, unwrap it and divide it into eight pieces. Roll one piece at a time into a ball. On a piece of the prepared parchment paper, use a rolling pin to flatten each piece of dough into a 5-inch (13-cm) disc, ¹⁄₁₆ inch (2 mm) thick.

Heat up the oil in a frying pan over low heat. Peel the parchment from a tortilla and cook it until golden, 1 to 2 minutes per side. As each tortilla is cooked, add it to an ovenproof plate, cover it with a tea towel and put the plate in the oven to keep the tortillas warm.

For the filling, divide the beans, cheese, avocado, paprika, salt, pepper, crème fraîche, if using, and salsa among four of the tortillas. Top the remaining tortillas with the filling and salsa, then serve the tacos immediately.

NOTE

The tortillas can be made up to 3 days ahead. Store them in an airtight container in the refrigerator. Warm them up in a frying pan for just a minute when you're ready to eat them.

ASPARAGUS, EGGS AND DREAMY LEMON DRIZZLE

Gone are the sugar-laden, glucose-spiking meals of a week ago. In their place are healthy protein- and fiber-rich breakfasts, loaded with vitamins, minerals and good fats. This breakfast is super simple to make, and the star of the plate is the lemony drizzle, made using anchovies, which are packed with heart-loving omega-3 fatty acids. It's also bursting with flavor. Crushed hazelnuts, which help regulate blood sugar, round off the drizzle perfectly.

Serves 4

4 large eggs

1 tsp plus ¼ cup (65 ml) olive or hazelnut oil, divided

1¾ cups (250 g) asparagus tips

¼ cup (29 g) whole hazelnuts

Juice of half a lemon

1½ oz (40 g) anchovies, finely chopped

1 tbsp (4 g) chopped fresh parsley

Salt and pepper, to taste

Bring a medium saucepan of water to a boil for your eggs. Add the eggs to the boiling water and cook them for 5 minutes for a soft-boiled egg or 9 minutes for hard-boiled.

In a frying pan, heat 1 teaspoon of the oil over medium heat. Add the asparagus, and fry them for 3 to 5 minutes, or until they are tender but still have a bit of bite.

While the asparagus fry, make the drizzle. Coarsely chop the hazelnuts, and put them in a medium bowl. Add the lemon juice, anchovies, parsley and remaining ¼ cup (60 ml) of olive oil, and whisk together until the ingredients are well combined. Add salt and pepper, to taste, and whisk again.

Peel the boiled eggs, and cut them in half lengthwise. Divide the asparagus among four plates, top them with the eggs, drizzle the dressing over everything, then serve.

LUNCH

Lunch times can be a real minefield when you're trying to avoid blood sugar–spiking foods. The standard lunch options tend to be mostly carb-focused—a sandwich, bowl of pasta, a baked potato—all the foods that convert to sugar in the body.

Have you ever eaten your lunch and felt completely wiped out an hour later? This is a blood sugar slump, and it's so common in the midafternoon that it is almost a daily occurrence for many people. Eliminating certain foods and instead eating nutritious meals that slowly release energy can prevent these slumps. Think of the process as nourishment, not punishment. You're eating the foods that are going to best energize you; you aren't depriving yourself.

The typical lunch break is 1 hour, so lunch needs to be quick and easy to make, filling and energy-boosting. The lunch options in this chapter will nourish and satiate. Plus, they're big on flavor and packed with goodness to keep you powering through your afternoons and well into the evening.

SPICY LENTIL SOUP

Fiber is such an important—and often overlooked—part of our diet that we should include in every meal, as it helps keep blood sugar levels steady, makes us feel full and aids our digestion, all of which are especially important during the cleanse, when we are changing our eating habits. All lentils are an excellent source of fiber, and they're also wonderfully easy to cook. This Spicy Lentil Soup is a one-pot wonder: It's a delicious lunch that's filling without being too heavy for an afternoon meal. Make extra to freeze for quick midweek lunches!

Serves 2

1 tbsp (15 ml) olive oil

1 onion, finely chopped

5 cloves garlic, minced

2 ribs celery, finely sliced

1 large red chile pepper, finely chopped

2 cups (400 g) cooked French lentils

½ cup (32 g) chopped fresh parsley, plus more for serving

1½ cups (24 g) chopped fresh cilantro, plus more for serving

1 tbsp (7 g) smoked paprika

1 tsp cayenne pepper

1 tsp cumin

6 cups (1.4 L) vegetable stock

Salt, to taste

Heat the oil over medium heat in a heavy-bottomed saucepan.

Add the onion and cook it for 5 minutes, until it turns translucent and light brown. Add the garlic, celery and chile, and cook them for 3 minutes, or until the ingredients soften.

Add the lentils, parsley, cilantro, paprika, cayenne and cumin and stir until the ingredients are well combined. Add the stock and salt, to taste. Keep stirring while bringing the mixture to a boil, then reduce the heat and simmer the soup for 25 to 30 minutes, or until the soup has thickened.

Serve with a sprinkle of cilantro and parsley.

QUINOA AND GOAT CHEESE BURGERS

It's great to get your protein during this cleanse from a number of sources, and the plant-based protein quinoa has the added benefit of high fiber content, too. Quinoa is a powerhouse of antioxidants and minerals, and it contains the full spectrum of the nine essential amino acids that must come from food, as the body can't make them. Quinoa is also great for metabolic function and improves blood sugar levels—making it perfect for rebounding from your sugar addiction. Healthy attributes aside, this gluten-free grain lends itself perfectly to this recipe, which can be made in bulk and stored in the freezer for up to two weeks. These burgers can be eaten hot or cold, and they are delicious as a nutritious stand-alone meal or served with salad.

Serves 4

2 medium carrots, grated

2 medium zucchinis, grated

1⅔ cups (300 g) cooked quinoa

2½ cups (40 g) chopped fresh cilantro

6 tbsp (24 g) chopped fresh parsley

1 large egg, beaten

1 tsp salt

3½ oz (100 g) goat cheese

¼ cup (30 g) buckwheat flour

2 tsp (10 ml) coconut or olive oil

Wrap the carrots and zucchini in muslin, cheesecloth or paper towels and place the package in a colander for 20 minutes to drain off as much of the liquid as possible. Remove the package from the colander, and give it another squeeze with your hands to make sure all of the liquid has been drained.

In a large mixing bowl, combine the carrots and zucchini with the quinoa, cilantro, parsley, egg and salt. Crumble in the goat cheese and flour, and mix until the ingredients are well combined. Shape the mixture into eight patties.

Heat the oil over low to medium heat in a frying pan, and cook the burgers for 4 to 5 minutes per side, or until they're nicely browned on both sides. Serve the burgers warm, or refrigerate them to eat later.

SATAY CHICKEN AND RAINBOW SALAD

This is a delicious lunch with visual appeal—from the vivid, vibrant colors—that also really delivers with taste. More than that, though, this meal introduces the bitter flavor profile; bitter foods stimulate the digestive process and help release enzymes to better digest proteins and fats. Since eating a high-sugar diet can impede digestive health and the ability to absorb key nutrients, incorporating bitter and pungent foods like the fresh ginger and cilantro in this recipe can help reduce inflammation and aid your digestive system overall. Enjoy this salad and chicken warm or chilled.

Serves 4

CHICKEN

1 tbsp (15 ml) coconut oil

1 tbsp (6 g) curry powder

18 oz (500 g) boneless skinless chicken breasts, cut into strips

RAINBOW SALAD

Juice of 1 lime

1 tsp fish sauce

1 tbsp (15 ml) soy sauce or liquid aminos

1¾ cups (125 g) shredded red cabbage (about ½ cabbage)

2 medium red bell peppers, julienned

2 medium carrots, julienned

1 chile pepper, diced

1¾ cups (28 g) chopped fresh cilantro

2 tbsp (20 g) peanuts, crushed

SATAY SAUCE

Juice of half a lime

1 tbsp (15 ml) soy sauce or liquid aminos

¼ cup (64 g) sugar-free smooth peanut butter

1 tbsp (15 ml) fish sauce

1 tsp grated ginger

1 clove garlic, minced

3 tbsp (45 ml) coconut milk

For the chicken, heat the coconut oil over medium heat in a frying pan; add the curry powder and stir it for a minute, until it starts to release its aroma. Add the chicken and fry it over medium heat for 10 minutes, or until there is no sign of redness when you cut into the thickest piece and it's golden brown.

For the salad, in a large bowl, whisk together the lime juice, fish sauce and soy sauce. Add the cabbage, bell peppers, carrots, chile, cilantro and peanuts. Toss the veggies to coat them with the dressing, then set the bowl aside to let the veggies marinate.

To make the sauce, in a jar whisk together the lime juice, soy sauce, peanut butter, fish sauce, ginger, garlic and coconut milk. Add a little water, if necessary, to make a smooth paste.

For serving, divide the salad among four plates, top it with the chicken and drizzle the satay sauce over all.

EASY, BREEZY BROCCOLI AND PESTO SOUP

This recipe could be called the "Super Greens Soup," because of its incredible fortifying ingredients. Broccoli alone has a cornucopia of health benefits: It has anti-inflammatory properties and heart-healthy antioxidants, and it's a fiber powerhouse. It aids digestive health, fights free radicals and is thought to slow the release of sugar into the bloodstream. When eliminating sugar from your diet, it's important to replace it with foods that can help restore health and vitality, making you less likely to crave high-sugar foods that release energy quickly. This is a great example of a simple recipe that does exactly that.

Serves 2

1 tbsp (15 g) butter

1 medium onion, roughly chopped

1 leek, roughly chopped

12 oz (335 g) broccoli, cut into florets

3 cloves garlic, chopped, divided

¼ cup (34 g) pine nuts, cashews or hemp seeds, divided, plus more for serving

3 cups (720 ml) chicken or vegetable stock

3 tbsp (45 ml) olive oil

1 oz (30 g) Parmesan cheese

1¼ cups (28 g) chopped fresh basil

Juice of half a lemon

Salt and pepper, to taste

2 tbsp (30 ml) cream, to top (optional)

Fresh basil leaves, torn, to top

Melt the butter in a soup pan, then add the onion and leek and fry them for 5 minutes, or until they are golden. Add the broccoli, two-thirds of the garlic and half of the pine nuts, and cook them on medium heat for 2 minutes, or until the ingredients have softened slightly. Pour in the stock and simmer the mixture for 15 minutes.

In a mini food processor, process the oil, remaining garlic and pine nuts, the Parmesan, basil and lemon juice, until the pesto is a smooth paste.

With an immersion blender, blend the broccoli and leeks until the soup is creamy, then cook it on medium heat for 3 to 5 minutes, or until it's bubbling slightly. Season the soup with the salt and pepper.

For serving, stir a couple of spoonfuls of pesto through the soup, then top each serving with pine nuts, an optional drizzle of cream and the torn basil.

CURRY SWEET POTATO CAKES

After a few days on the cleanse, you will start to notice how much your palate has changed. You should be able to really taste food again without sugar addiction clouding your taste buds. The sweet potato in this recipe will taste amazing, enhanced by the spices and sharpness of the lemon. The combination of ingredients in this healthy, plant-based, high-protein meal will trigger all of your taste receptors.

Serves 4

CURRY SWEET POTATO CAKES

1½ lbs (600 g) sweet potatoes, cut into small chunks

1 tsp salt, divided

2 tsp (10 ml) coconut oil, divided

1 medium red onion, chopped

3 cloves garlic, minced

2 tbsp (13 g) curry powder

1 tbsp (6 g) garam masala

½ tsp chili powder

1¾ cups (28 g) chopped fresh cilantro

1 large egg, beaten

1½ cups (250 g) drained and rinsed canned chickpeas

3½ tbsp (28 g) chickpea flour, plus more, if needed

SPICED YOGURT DIPPING SAUCE

1 tbsp (1 g) finely chopped fresh cilantro

1 clove garlic, grated

⅓ cup (80 ml) plain full-fat Greek yogurt

½ tsp cayenne pepper

1 tsp harissa paste

1 tbsp (15 ml) lemon juice

Salt and pepper, to taste

For the potato cakes, bring a large saucepan of water to a boil. Add the sweet potatoes and half the salt to the water, and boil the potatoes for 8 to 10 minutes, or until they are soft when pierced with a knife. Drain the potatoes.

While the potatoes are boiling, heat half of the coconut oil in a frying pan on low to medium heat, then add the onion and sauté for 5 minutes, or until it is translucent, then add the garlic, curry powder, garam masala, chili powder and cilantro, and fry for 2 to 3 minutes, or until they become aromatic.

Empty the sautéed onion mixture into a mixing bowl, and add the cooked potatoes, egg, chickpeas, chickpea flour and the remaining salt. Thoroughly mash the ingredients until everything's well combined and there are no lumps, then shape the mixture into eight patties.

Add the remaining coconut oil to a frying pan and cook the patties over low to medium heat for 10 minutes, turning halfway through, until both sides are browned. You may have to cook the patties in two batches to keep them in a single layer and avoid overcrowding the pan.

Make the dipping sauce while the potato cakes are cooking. In a small bowl, combine the cilantro, garlic, yogurt, cayenne, harissa and lemon juice. Season the dip to taste with the salt and pepper, and stir again.

Serve the potato cakes with the dip.

CHICKPEA AND MUSHROOM STROGANOFF

This lunch is a delicious recipe that takes just 15 minutes to make. Both mushrooms and chickpeas absorb flavors and lend texture while providing protein, fiber and antioxidants. Chickpeas also help to reduce blood sugar and improve gut health, owing to their fiber content. Eating a high-sugar diet can lead to gut dysbiosis, which causes sugar cravings in the short term and more serious health concerns in the longer term. So, it's important to eat restorative, healthy meals like these to cultivate a healthy gut microbiome.

Serves 4

1 tbsp (15 ml) olive oil

1 medium onion, diced

4 cloves garlic, minced

1½ lbs (680 g) mushrooms, sliced or diced

½ cup (32 g) chopped fresh parsley, plus more for serving

1 tbsp (7 g) smoked paprika

2½ cups (425 g) drained and rinsed canned chickpeas

⅔ cup (160 ml) vegetable stock

⅓ cup (80 ml) sour cream

Salt and pepper, to taste

Heat the oil over medium heat in a frying pan, then add the onion and sauté it for 5 minutes, or until it is translucent. Then, add the garlic, mushrooms, parsley and paprika and cook the mixture, stirring, for 2 minutes, or until the ingredients soften.

Add the chickpeas, and pour in the stock. As the stock reduces a little and starts to bubble, reduce the heat to a simmer and stir in the sour cream. Season the mixture with the salt and pepper, and stir again. Simmer the mixture for 2 minutes, or until it's slightly thickened.

Ladle the stroganoff into four bowls, and garnish it with the parsley.

CHILI BLACK BEAN SOUP

Switching from processed to real food will massively reduce sugar cravings, because you help create a homeostasis in your body, which will enable you to function more optimally. A simple meal like this soup is big on flavor and hits all the nutritional needs. Black beans are a great plant-based protein that help stave off cravings and boost fiber intake. Adding avocado, a raw chile pepper and garlic provides healthy fat, nutrients and vitamins.

Serves 4

SOUP

1 tbsp (15 ml) olive oil

2 large onions, finely chopped

5 cloves garlic, minced

3 cups (48 g) chopped fresh cilantro, divided

2 red chile peppers, chopped

1 tbsp (5 g) ground coriander

2 tbsp (14 g) paprika

Salt and pepper, to taste

4¾ cups (800 g) drained and rinsed canned black beans

3 cups (720 ml) vegetable stock

9 oz (250 g) passata

GUACAMOLE

1 avocado, roughly chopped, divided

1 clove garlic, minced

⅔ cup (5 g) finely chopped fresh cilantro

1 chile pepper, sliced

Juice of 1 lime

Pinch of salt

FOR SERVING

Sour cream

Cilantro, torn, to garnish

1 lime, sliced

For the soup, in a heavy-bottomed pan, heat the oil over medium heat, add the onions and cook them for 5 minutes, or until they're translucent. Add the garlic, half of the cilantro, the chiles, coriander, paprika, salt and pepper, and give everything a good stir. Cook the mixture for 2 minutes, then add the beans and stock, and simmer the mixture over low heat for 5 minutes. Stir in the passata and remaining cilantro. Simmer the soup for 15 minutes.

Make the guacamole while the soup cooks. In a small bowl, combine the avocado, garlic, cilantro, chile and lime juice. Season with the salt, and mash the mixture until it's nice and smooth.

For serving, ladle the soup into bowls, and top it with dollops of chunky guacamole, sour cream, cilantro and slices of lime. Serve immediately.

DINNER

This is the time of day that you should start to unwind and trigger your body's "rest and digest" process, or *parasympathetic nervous system*. The key word here is "digest." How you eat is as important as what you eat. For example, if you're mindlessly shoveling your food down, you are not giving your body the chance to properly activate the digestive system, which is key to how your body assimilates and absorbs the incoming nutrients. And a lack of nutrients can lead to cravings!

We often hear about eating mindfully, but do we actually know why it's so critical? When we eat mindfully, pause between each mouthful and chew properly, we are allowing our digestive system to do its thing. We also create space for the brain-stomach signals to be sent and received, which helps us register feelings of fullness, reducing the risk of overeating.

What we eat at the end of the day is, of course, paramount. Eating sugary foods before bed disrupts sleep. It also leaves us tired and inclined to crave and eat more sugary or starchy foods the next day.

Post–evening meal seems to be one of the most common times for cravings to hit, so the dinners in this chapter are designed to be simple to execute and to use varied flavors that help dampen evening cravings. I've created meals with lots of variety, to keep things interesting and avoid menu fatigue. You'll be able to savor lots of different spices, herbs and blends and lots of texture, too, with recipes that will become family favorites.

TURKEY AND HARISSA BURGERS WITH LIME AND CILANTRO BROWN RICE

The word "carbohydrate" seems to have become a dirty word among dieters. But not all carbs are created equal. Take brown rice: The nutty whole grain has numerous health benefits and promotes fullness, while keeping blood sugar levels steady. It also pairs perfectly with these succulent, flavorsome turkey burgers that are high in protein, tryptophan, vitamin B and minerals. That makes these burgers an ideal meal for satiety and curbing your sugar cravings!

Serves 4

1¼ cups (250 g) brown rice

2 tsp (12 g) salt, divided

18 oz (500 g) ground turkey

1 red chile pepper, finely chopped

2 cups (90 g) chopped scallions

2 cloves garlic, minced

1½ cups (24 g) chopped fresh cilantro, divided

1 egg, beaten

2 tbsp (30 ml) fish sauce

2 tbsp (30 g) harissa paste, plus more for serving

Juice of 1 lime, divided

2 tbsp (30 ml) coconut oil, divided

1 tbsp (15 ml) soy sauce or liquid aminos

Plain full-fat Greek yogurt

Lime wedges

Cook the brown rice as the package directs, adding 1 teaspoon of the salt to the water.

In a large mixing bowl, mix together the turkey, chile, scallions, garlic and half of the cilantro. In a jar, whisk together the egg, fish sauce, harissa, half of the lime juice, half of the coconut oil and the remaining 1 teaspoon of salt. Pour the mixture into the ground meat mixture, and mix until it's well combined.

Shape the mixture into four patties, and refrigerate them for 15 minutes to firm them. Heat the remaining coconut oil over low heat in a large frying pan, then add the patties. Cover the pan and cook the patties for 12 to 15 minutes, or until they are nicely browned; flip the patties halfway through the cooking time.

While your turkey burgers are cooking, drain the rice, if needed, then stir in the soy sauce, together with the remaining lime juice and cilantro.

Serve the turkey burgers with the rice, topped with harissa, yogurt and a squeeze of lime.

PULLED HOT SAUCE CHICKEN WITH SWEET POTATO AND CHUNKY GUAC

Eating a sugary diet can drown out other flavors, but there's nothing like capsaicin—found in chile peppers—to get taste buds fired up. Like sugar, capsaicin is also known to trigger the feel-good hormone serotonin. Because spicy food does not cause cravings like sugar does, eating it is a healthy way to get the same feel-good boost without the sugar negatives. This hot sauce is a taste sensation: hot, piquant and banging with flavor. This wonderfully nutritious dinner has immune system and mood-boosting properties.

HOT SAUCE

15 red chile peppers (Fresno or cayenne are good options)

2 tbsp (30 g) butter

2 white onions, roughly chopped

4 cloves garlic, chopped

5 ripe plum tomatoes, chopped

1 tbsp (6 g) chili powder

1 tbsp (7 g) smoked paprika

Salt, to taste

½ cup (120 ml) apple cider vinegar

CHICKEN

18 oz (500 g) boneless skinless chicken breasts

1 tbsp (15 g) butter

2 medium red onions, thinly sliced

3 tbsp (6 g) chopped fresh cilantro

⅔ cup (160 ml) Hot Sauce (see Note)

1 tsp salt, divided

3 cups (300 g) diced sweet potatoes

1 tsp olive oil

For the sauce, sterilize a jar and funnel, and set them aside. Put on rubber gloves if you have them, because no one wants to touch their eyes or any other sensitive body parts with hands that handled hot peppers.

Halve the chiles; remove the seeds if you prefer milder sauce. Melt the butter over high heat in a frying pan, then add the chiles, onions, garlic, tomatoes, chili powder, paprika and salt. Cook the mixture, stirring continuously, for 5 minutes, until the vegetables begin to soften.

Stir in the apple cider vinegar. Take the pan off the heat, and carefully pour the sauce mixture into a blender; blend until the ingredients are well-incorporated. If you want a really smooth sauce, pour it through a sieve. Use the funnel to pour the sauce into the sanitized jar. Add the lid. You can process the hot sauce in a water bath canner for shelf storage for up to a year. Or, let it cool, then pop it in the fridge, where it will keep for a week or two.

For the chicken, preheat the oven to 370°F (185°C, gas mark 5). Place the chicken on a rimmed baking sheet with the butter, onions and the cilantro. Pour the Hot Sauce over the mixture, and sprinkle it with half a teaspoon of the salt. Cook the chicken in the oven for 20 minutes, or until the juices run clear. Make an incision in the thickest part of the chicken to make sure the meat is white all the way through, with no sign of redness.

Arrange the sweet potatoes on a rimmed baking sheet, then drizzle them with the oil and sprinkle on the remaining half a teaspoon of salt. When the chicken has been cooking for 5 minutes, put the sweet potatoes in the oven for 15 minutes, or until the edges have browned and the inside is soft when pierced with a fork.

(continued)

PULLED HOT SAUCE CHICKEN WITH SWEET POTATO AND CHUNKY GUAC (CONTINUED)

CHUNKY GUAC

2 avocados, chopped into big chunks

Juice of 1 lemon

3 tbsp (6 g) chopped fresh cilantro

Salt, to taste

FOR SERVING

2 limes, cut into wedges

Chopped fresh cilantro

1 medium red chile pepper, sliced

Make the Chunky Guac while the chicken and potatoes cook. Roughly stir together the avocados, lemon juice, cilantro and a sprinkle of salt.

Remove the chicken from the oven, and shred the fillets, using two forks. Make sure you mop up all the juices and remaining sauce with the shreds—the chicken should be well coated in the sauce.

For serving, divide the chicken and sweet potatoes among four plates, add a side of the guac, the limes, cilantro and red chile.

NOTE

To save time, you can use a store-bought hot sauce instead of my Hot Sauce; just make sure it's one without sugar.

MOZZARELLA BEEF MEATBALLS AND GARLIC CAULI RICE

So many meatball recipes are loaded with white breadcrumbs that spike blood sugar. This recipe replaces the bread with Parmesan, for a wonderful depth of flavor with far less sugar. I smother these in a rich, non-starchy tomato sauce that oozes with lip-smacking, umami tastiness, which is exactly what's needed from a meal when you are trying to distract from sugar cravings.

Serves 4

MEATBALLS

1 tsp plus 1 tbsp (20 ml) olive oil, divided

1 medium onion, finely chopped

1 clove garlic, minced

1 lb (455 g) ground beef

1 tsp onion powder

1 tsp garlic powder

1 tsp dried thyme

1 tsp dried oregano

¼ cup (25 g) grated Parmesan cheese

1 tsp salt

1 tsp pepper

2 tbsp (30 ml) Worcestershire sauce

2 large eggs, beaten

¼ lb (115 g) mozzarella, cut into 24 small cubes

SAUCE

1 tsp olive oil

1 medium onion, finely chopped

3 cloves garlic, crushed

1 tsp dried oregano

½ cup (30 g) finely chopped sun-dried tomatoes

1 cup (240 ml) chicken or vegetable stock

18 oz (500 g) passata

1 tbsp (15 ml) full-fat milk or cream (see Note)

1 cup (24 g) chopped fresh basil

Salt and pepper, to taste

For the meatballs, heat the 1 teaspoon of oil over medium heat in a frying pan. Add the onion and cook it for 5 minutes, until it turns translucent, then add the garlic and cook it for 2 minutes. Remove the mixture from the heat and set it aside to cool slightly.

In a large mixing bowl, place the beef, onion and garlic powders, thyme, oregano, Parmesan, salt, pepper, Worcestershire sauce, eggs and slightly cooled onion mixture. Thoroughly mix together the ingredients until the meat is completely ground and all the ingredients are blended. The more ground the meat is, the more succulent the meatballs will be.

Tear off 24 walnut-sized pieces of the mixture, stuff each piece with a chunk of mozzarella, then seal it and roll it into a ball. When you've finished making the meatballs, pop them in the fridge to firm them up.

For the sauce, heat the oil in a saucepan over medium heat, add the onion and cook it for 5 minutes, until translucent. Add the garlic, oregano and sun-dried tomatoes. Little by little, pour in the stock, and cook the mixture for 5 to 7 minutes to let it reduce and thicken between additions of stock. Pour in the passata and milk and stir, then add the basil. Simmer the sauce gently, over low heat, for about 15 minutes.

Remove the meatballs from the fridge. Heat the remaining 1 tablespoon (15 ml) of olive oil in a frying pan over medium heat. Then, add the meatballs, a few at a time, and cook them for roughly 6 minutes, until they are nicely browned; turn them to make sure all sides are browned. Cut into one of the larger meatballs; if it's brown all the way through, they're cooked. Then, add the meatballs to the simmering tomato sauce. Repeat this until all your meatballs are cooked and sitting in the tomato sauce. Add any juices from the meatball pan to the sauce and season with salt and pepper to taste.

(continued)

MOZZARELLA BEEF MEATBALLS AND GARLIC CAULI RICE (CONTINUED)

GARLIC CAULI RICE

1½ heads of cauliflower, roughly chopped

¼ cup (16 g) chopped fresh parsley

1 tbsp (15 g) butter

1 clove garlic, minced

FOR SERVING

Fresh basil leaves, torn

For the cauli rice, process the cauliflower and parsley in a food processor until it's the consistency of couscous. In another frying pan, melt the butter over low heat. Add the cauliflower and parsley mixture and the garlic, and cook the rice for a few minutes, or until the cauli starts to catch ever so slightly on the pan.

For serving, divide the cauli rice among four plates, top it with six meatballs on each plate, then ladle the sauce over all. Garnish the plate with the torn basil.

NOTE

Milk will dim the metallic taste that sometimes occurs with cooking tomatoes; cream will provide richer flavor.

SAGE PORK CUTLETS WITH BUTTERY SWEET POTATO MASH

This recipe uses incredibly simple ingredients to jazz up the tired meat and veg combo. Sage is an herb that's mostly associated with turkey stuffing, but there's so much more to this garden perennial. Sage is renowned for its health benefits, including lowering insulin sensitivity. Adding it to pork makes a divine pairing, and, with a buttery sweet potato mash on the side, you've got a brand-new comfort food that's super simple to rustle up and healthy, too.

Serves 4

Pinches of salt, divided

4 large sweet potatoes, chopped

¾ cup (30 g) fresh sage, several leaves reserved for garnish, the rest roughly chopped

1 clove garlic, grated

3 tbsp (45 g) butter, divided

Pinches of pepper, divided

4 pork loin chops (17 oz [480 g])

1 tsp freshly grated nutmeg

Preheat the oven to 400°F (200°C, gas mark 6).

Bring a saucepan of water to a boil. Add a pinch of the salt and the sweet potatoes; the water should completely cover the potatoes. Boil the potatoes for 10 minutes, or until they are tender when pierced with a knife. Drain the potatoes and return them to the pan.

In a small bowl, use a spoon to blend together the chopped sage, garlic, half of the butter, a pinch of salt and a pinch of pepper.

With a sharp knife, score the fat on the pork in a crisscross pattern, only cutting halfway down the thickness of the fat. Rub the sage butter into the scored fat and both sides of the chops. Bake the chops on a baking sheet for 15 minutes, or until an instant-read thermometer inserted into the center of the meat registers 145°F (63°C).

While the chops are roasting, add the remaining half of the butter to the boiled sweet potatoes in the pan and mash them together; season the potatoes with salt and pepper. Add the nutmeg, and warm the potatoes through over very low heat, about 3 to 4 minutes, making sure they don't stick to the bottom of the pan. Remove the chops from the oven and let them rest for 3 minutes.

Serve the chops and mashed sweet potatoes, garnished with the sage leaves.

PARMA HAM AND ARUGULA CAULI PIZZA

Who doesn't love a pizza with tangy, herby tomato sauce and stringy melted mozzarella? You can have your pizza and eat it, too, during this sugar cleanse! We're swapping out the stodgy dough for a Parmesan cheesy cauli-crust that's bristling with flavor before you've even added the toppings. There won't be any carb crash after eating this, either. Instead, you'll be full up on delicious fortifying ingredients.

Serves 4

TOMATO SAUCE

½ white onion, chopped into eighths

2 cloves garlic, chopped

½ chile pepper, chopped (optional)

4 red beefsteak tomatoes, chopped into quarters

⅓ cup (8 g) fresh basil leaves

Pinch of salt

1 tsp olive oil

½ tsp chili flakes

1 tsp dried oregano

2 tbsp (32 g) tomato paste

1 tsp Worcestershire sauce

CAULIFLOWER BASE

1½ heads of cauliflower, roughly chopped

⅔ cup (66 g) grated Parmesan

½ cup (50 g) finely ground almond flour

2 large eggs

1 tbsp (15 ml) olive oil

1 tsp garlic powder

1 tsp onion powder

Pinch of salt

TOPPING

2⅓ cups (150 g) sliced mozzarella

2½ oz (70 g) torn prosciutto

¼ cup (40 g) diced tomatoes

⅛ cup (20 g) pitted and halved black olives

¾ cup (18 g) fresh basil leaves

1 red onion, sliced

2 cups (40 g) arugula

Preheat the oven to 325°F (165°C, gas mark 3).

For the pizza sauce, place the onion, garlic, chile, if using, tomatoes and basil on a baking sheet. Sprinkle the vegetables with the salt, and drizzle them with the oil. Roast the mixture in the oven for 15 minutes, or until the vegetables are tender.

Make the cauliflower base while the vegetables roast. In a food processor, blend the cauliflower until it's a fine consistency. Empty it onto a muslin cloth or dish towel, and squeeze out any liquid. Place the dry cauliflower in a mixing bowl, and combine it with the Parmesan, almond flour, eggs, olive oil, garlic powder, onion powder and salt. When it's fully mixed, spoon the mixture out onto parchment paper or a pizza tray, if you have one. Press the mixture down into four round bases, each the size of an open hand. Bake the crusts for 15 minutes, until they crisp a little.

To finish the tomato sauce, remove the veggies from the oven, and pour them into a blender. Add the chili flakes, oregano, tomato paste and Worcestershire sauce, and blend until you have a smooth sauce.

Remove the cauliflower bases from the oven, and spoon the sauce on them. Layer the bases with the mozzarella, prosciutto, tomatoes, olives, basil and onion. Return the pizzas to the oven for 5 minutes, until the cheese is fully melted. Serve the pizzas with a handful of arugula on each.

TANDOORI CHICKEN AND PANEER KEBABS

I'm all for re-creating beloved takeout foods and making them with healthy, nutritious ingredients instead. This meal is loaded with protein, fiber and vitamins, and the super side salad is jam-packed with anti-inflammatory anthocyanins, which will help heal your body from inflammation caused by excessive sugar consumption. As well as tasting delicious, the fragrant Indian spices and herbs used for these kebabs are also known for their anti-inflammatory properties. This meal serves up a myriad of flavors that really pop and satiate any appetite.

CHICKEN

Juice of half a lemon

⅓ cup (80 ml) plain full-fat Greek yogurt

2 tbsp (2 g) chopped fresh cilantro

2 cloves garlic, minced

½-inch (1.3-cm) piece of ginger, grated

3 tbsp (19 g) tandoori spice

½ tsp salt

1 lb (450 g) boneless skinless chicken breasts, cubed

3 cups (200 g) halved mushrooms

1⅓ cups (200 g) paneer cheese, cubed

1 red bell pepper, cut into thick pieces

1 zucchini, cut into thick slices

2 small red onions, each cut lengthwise into 8 wedges

16 (8-inch [20-cm]) skewers, soaked in water for 5 minutes if wooden

SUPER SIDE SALAD

2 cups (140 g) shredded red cabbage

½ cucumber, grated into long, thick ribbons

5 cups (80 g) chopped fresh cilantro

Juice of half a lemon

1½ tbsp (20 ml) olive oil

1 tsp chili flakes

Pinch of salt

Preheat the oven to 370°F (185°C, gas mark 5).

For the chicken, in a large mixing bowl, mix the lemon juice, yogurt, cilantro, garlic, ginger, tandoori spice and salt until it's well combined. Next add the chicken, ensure it's completely covered in the sauce, cover the bowl and refrigerate it for 30 minutes to marinate (see Tips).

Remove the chicken from the fridge, and thread a chunk of chicken, a mushroom, paneer cube, bell pepper piece, zucchini slice and onion piece onto a skewer. Be careful not to pack the pieces on too tightly, as this can prevent even cooking. Repeat to make 16 skewers.

Arrange the skewers across two baking sheets so they can cook evenly, and roast them in the oven for 20 minutes, until the meat is white all the way through, with no sign of redness when you cut into one of the largest pieces. Turn the skewers every 5 minutes during cooking, so they brown evenly and cook on all sides.

If you don't have skewers, you can prepare the chicken, paneer and the veggies the same way, just arrange the pieces on a wire rack over a baking sheet. Turn the pieces every 5 minutes to make sure they're evenly cooked.

Make the salad while the chicken kebabs are cooking. In a large serving bowl, mix together the cabbage, cucumber, cilantro, lemon juice, oil, chili flakes and salt.

Serve the skewers on a large plate or chopping board, alongside the salad.

TIPS

You will need to marinate the chicken for 30 minutes minimum, but I suggest marinating it for a couple of hours, if you have the time to plan ahead. When prepping the veggies and paneer, cut them roughly the same chunky size as the chicken, so they can be threaded on the skewers easily.

LAMB KOFTAS AND MINT YOGURT DIP

I used garam masala in this meal for its incredible aromatic flavors and because this wonderfully grounding and warming spice blend is thought to lower cholesterol and blood sugar levels. It's a great dish to establish new flavors that help to reduce sugar cravings. It's also said to aid digestion and boost the metabolism. This is a quick dinner that can be made in advance since the koftas freeze well. The cooling, gut-loving mint and yogurt complements the koftas stunningly.

LAMB KOFTAS

2 cloves garlic

1 large white onion, roughly chopped

3 tbsp (25 g) pine nuts, plus a few more for garnish

¼ cup (24 g) chopped fresh mint, plus a few leaves for garnish

1½ cups (24 g) chopped fresh cilantro

2 tbsp (12 g) garam masala

1 tbsp (5 g) ground coriander

1 tbsp (5 g) chili powder

1 tsp cumin

½ tsp turmeric

21 oz (600 g) ground lamb

1 tbsp (15 ml) olive oil, plus more for baking

Pinch of salt

1 tbsp (8 g) garlic powder

8 (8-inch [20-cm]) skewers, soaked in water for 5 minutes if wooden

MINT YOGURT DIP

½ cup (120 ml) plain full-fat Greek yogurt

Juice of half a lemon

¼ cup (24 g) chopped fresh mint

Preheat the oven to 370°F (185°C, gas mark 5), and place a wire rack over a rimmed baking sheet.

For the koftas, in a food processor, pulse the garlic, onion, pine nuts, mint, cilantro, garam masala, coriander, chili powder, cumin and turmeric until the mixture is the consistency of a chunky paste.

In a large mixing bowl, grind together with your hands the lamb, oil and salt, really breaking down the meat. Add the spice and fresh herb mixture to the meat, along with the garlic powder, and combine it thoroughly. Shape the mixture into eight sausage-shaped koftas, and refrigerate them for 15 minutes to firm them.

For the dip, whisk together the yogurt, lemon juice and mint until well combined. Refrigerate the dip until you serve the koftas.

Remove the koftas from the fridge, and put a skewer through the bottom of each one. Put the koftas on the prepared rack, and drizzle them with olive oil. Bake the koftas for 12 minutes, or until they are well-browned on the outside and there is no sign of redness inside. If you're not using skewers, place the oiled koftas directly on the wire rack. Turn the koftas every 5 minutes to make sure they're evenly cooked.

Serve the koftas, garnished with mint leaves, a few pine nuts, the yogurt dip and with a side salad.

SNACKS

Hunger is your enemy while you are quitting sugar. So, fill up!

These snacks are all designed to inspire you to explore and fall in love with new flavors and textures far beyond sugar. I'm hoping that by the end of your cleanse, you'll end up craving these delicious and nutritious alternatives, instead of craving sugar! At every point of this cleanse, it's important to know that everything you are eating is as fortifying as it is tasty. These snacks are designed to optimize your health!

Having the right snacks can really help keep you on the no- or low-sugar path. That point in between your meals where you begin to feel a little peckish is the potential weak spot that could have you falling off the wagon and reaching for a chocolate bar or cookie. So rather than being caught short, be prepared with an arsenal of delicious snacks. Popcorn (page 77) is probably the easiest go-to of them all. It takes minutes to make, absorbs flavors, is inexpensive and, best of all, is so easy to pop in a container and eat on the go. Za'atar chickpeas (page 82) are a personal favorite of mine. They're like little flavor bombs and they stay fresh for 3 to 4 days, perfect for making up a batch in advance. My all-time favorite in this chapter, though, has to be the halloumi fries (page 81). They're a little more time-consuming to make but worth every second.

Feel free to make and eat as many of these snacks as you want during your sugar-free cleanse.

GOURMET POPCORN

What's movie night without the popcorn? We've got that covered with this selection of popcorn, with not a sugar-spiking syrup in sight. This is a sugar-free journey, and it's about unlearning what the marketing campaigns have brainwashed us with. Savory popcorn is a great alternative to caramel corn or popcorn paired with candy, and it doesn't just have to be butter and salt—go gourmet with tasty flavor pairings. Here's popcorn that's big on flavors, with your choice of three different toppings, and worthy of any sequel.

Serves 2-4

TRUFFLE OIL AND PARMESAN

1 tsp truffle oil

1 cup (100 g) grated Parmesan cheese

Salt, to taste

CINNAMON BUTTER

1 cup (240 ml) melted salted butter

1 tbsp (8 g) cinnamon

CHILI AND LIME

2 tbsp (30 ml) lime juice

2 tsp (12 g) chili powder

Salt and pepper, to taste

POPCORN

3 tbsp (45 ml) coconut oil

1 cup (125 g) popcorn kernels

For the truffle oil topping, in a small bowl stir together the oil, Parmesan and salt. Set aside the bowl while you cook the popcorn.

For the cinnamon topping, stir together the butter and cinnamon in a small bowl. Set aside the bowl while you cook the popcorn.

For the chili topping, combine the lime juice, chili powder, salt and pepper in a small bowl. Set aside the bowl while you cook the popcorn.

For the popcorn, melt the coconut oil over medium heat in a heavy-bottomed saucepan. Place two kernels into the oil to gauge the temperature. When the first kernel pops, the oil is hot enough.

Pour in the remainder of the kernels, and cover the pan with a lid, leaving a gap for steam to escape. Keep the pot moving to make sure that the kernels cook evenly. Cook the popcorn for about 3 minutes, or until the kernels stop popping. Remove the popcorn from the heat, and pour it into a large serving bowl. Add the reserved seasoning mix, and toss the popcorn to coat it.

COCONUT CHICKEN DIPPERS

Food is such a big part of our lives; it's only right it should be enjoyed. Sometimes, we crave that something naughty. What I'm all about is taking that something naughty, like chicken dippers, and transforming it into a healthy, utterly delicious snack that's nicer than the naughty! And what's a chicken dipper without a dip? The problem with many condiments is that they contain a lot of sugar and syrup. I've solved that problem with this tangy, sweet, smoky and sugar-free tomato sauce, which you can make by the batch to have on hand in the fridge.

Serves 4

CHICKEN DIPPERS

1 cup (128 g) arrowroot powder

3 large eggs, beaten

3 cups (300 g) unsweetened coconut flakes

2 tbsp (14 g) smoked paprika, divided

2 tbsp (11 g) cayenne pepper, divided

2 tbsp (17 g) garlic powder, divided

2 lbs (900 g) large boneless, skinless chicken breasts, butterflied and cut into uniform, bite-sized strips

1 tsp salt

1 tsp pepper

SPICY TOMATO DIP

2 tbsp (30 ml) olive oil

½ onion, roughly chopped

½ red apple, roughly chopped

1 small chile pepper, seeded and roughly chopped

Pinch of salt (optional), plus more, to taste

1 clove garlic, minced

2 tbsp (30 g) tomato puree

3 tbsp (45 g) passata

½ tsp cayenne pepper

3 tbsp (45 ml) white wine vinegar

½ tsp smoked paprika

½ tsp cinnamon

For the chicken, preheat the oven to 375°F (190°C, gas mark 5).

In three separate bowls, place the arrowroot powder, eggs and coconut. Add 1 tablespoon (7 g) of the paprika, 1 tablespoon (6 g) of the cayenne and 1 tablespoon (7 g) of garlic powder to the arrowroot; stir to combine. Add the remaining paprika, cayenne pepper and garlic powder to the eggs; stir to combine.

Dip the chicken strips into each bowl, beginning with the arrowroot, then the egg and finally the coconut, making sure all of the chicken is thoroughly coated. Arrange the strips on a rimmed baking sheet and sprinkle with the salt and pepper. Bake the chicken for 20 to 25 minutes, or until it's golden brown outside and white all the way through, with no sign of redness, when you cut into one of the largest pieces.

For the dip, heat the oil in a saucepan over medium-low heat, and add the onion, apple and chile. Gently sweat the ingredients for 10 minutes, or until the onion is translucent; you can season the onion with a pinch of salt to increase the speed of the process. Add the garlic, and cook it for 5 minutes. Then add the tomato puree, passata, cayenne pepper, vinegar, paprika, cinnamon and salt. Cook the mixture for 15 minutes, or until the sauce has thickened and reduced to the consistency of jam.

Transfer the mixture to a high-speed blender, and blend until the mixture is smooth. Strain the dip through a sieve; it can be refrigerated, ideally in glass jars, for up to a week.

Serve the chicken dippers warm from the oven with the Spicy Tomato Dip.

HALLOUMI FRIES AND YOGURT LIME DIP

I toyed with calling these "favorite fries," because they are truly one of the most appetizing snacks you can make. The coating has a sublime layer of crunch before giving way to the melting halloumi. Doing this sugar cleanse allows you to explore lots of new snacks and treats, expand your palate and help you move beyond your sugar cravings—one delicious fry at a time.

Serves 2-4

YOGURT LIME DIP

1¼ cups (300 ml) plain full-fat Greek yogurt

Juice of half a lime

1 tsp garlic powder

Fresh cilantro, for garnish (optional)

HALLOUMI FRIES

⅔ cup (85 g) arrowroot powder

2 tsp (4 g) paprika

Salt, to taste

½ cup (120 ml) melted coconut oil, for frying (more or less depending on pan size)

18 oz (500 g) block halloumi cheese, cut into strips

For the dip, in a bowl, mix the yogurt, lime juice and garlic powder. Refrigerate the dip while you make the fries.

For the halloumi, set a wire rack in a rimmed baking sheet.

Mix the arrowroot, paprika and salt on a medium-sized plate.

Pour about ¼ inch (6 mm) of oil into a deep-sided, heavy pan and heat the oil over medium-high heat. For a successful fry, aim for the oil to be at 375°F (190°C). If you don't have a thermometer, you can drop a small bit of water into the pan—if it evaporates immediately, your oil is ready to use.

Pat dry the strips of halloumi. Coat them evenly with the starch mixture, shaking off any excess. Depending on your pan size, put four or five fries into the hot oil, taking care to place the fries into the oil away from yourself. You don't want to overcrowd the pan, as this will bring the temperature of the oil down.

Fry the halloumi for 2 to 3 minutes per side, or until the halloumi is golden brown and crispy. Remove the finished fries and place them on the prepared wire rack. Immediately season the fries with salt to taste. Repeat the frying process until all of the halloumi is fried.

Serve the fries with the Yogurt Lime Dip, garnished with the cilantro, if using.

ROASTED ZA'ATAR CHICKPEAS

These fiber-dense, za'atar-roasted chickpeas are the perfect swap for unhealthy potato chips. We predominantly crave sugar and salt; the problem with that is, if we eat too much salt, we crave sugar, and vice versa. We need foods, like za'atar, that trigger savory tastes instead. Za'atar is a blend of herbs and spices with a full spectrum of flavor. Make lots of these chickpeas and store them, so you have a tasty, instant snack on hand.

Serves 2-4

ZA'ATAR SPICE BLEND

1 tbsp (5 g) ground coriander

1 tbsp (6 g) cumin

1 tbsp (3 g) dried oregano

1 tbsp (9 g) sesame seeds

1 tbsp (6 g) sumac

1 tbsp (18 g) kosher salt

CHICKPEAS

4 cups (680 g) drained and rinsed canned chickpeas

2 tbsp (30 ml) olive oil

Kosher salt, to taste

3 tbsp (42 g) Za'atar Spice Blend

Place a rack in the center of the oven and preheat it to 400°F (200°C, gas mark 6). Line a rimmed baking sheet with parchment paper.

To make the Za'atar Spice Blend, mix the coriander, cumin, oregano, sesame seeds, sumac and salt together in a bowl. The blend can be stored in an airtight, preferably glass, container.

For the chickpeas, in a large bowl, toss together the chickpeas, olive oil, salt and Za'atar Spice Blend, until the chickpeas are evenly coated. Let them marinate for 15 to 25 minutes.

Spread the chickpeas onto the prepared baking sheet. Bake the chickpeas in the center of the oven for 30 minutes, or until they are golden brown and crunchy; give the pan a little shake every 5 minutes to ensure even browning and crisping.

Allow the chickpeas to cool completely. Leftovers can be stored in an airtight container for up to a week.

TIP

To extract the best flavor, toast any whole seeds you may use before grinding them and adding them to recipes like the za'atar spice mix. Toast seeds over medium heat in a preheated skillet, stirring, until the seeds are lightly browned and/or aromatic.

SWEET CAULI CHEESE BITES

These are fluffy bites of sweet and savory satisfaction. They have so much texture, combining a deliciously light center with little bursts of crunchy quinoa flakes on the outside. I advise you to make big batches of these to keep in the fridge, then cook them as you go; store some in the freezer, too! Brimming with flavor, they really do hit the spot!

Serves 2-4

1 sweet potato (4 oz [115 g])

½ head of cauliflower, chopped

⅔ cup (66 g) grated Parmesan cheese, divided

1 tbsp (8 g) garlic powder

1 tbsp (3 g) mixed dried herbs, such as basil, oregano and parsley

Salt and pepper, to taste

½ cup (50 g) quinoa flakes

3 tbsp (22 g) buckwheat flour

½ tsp paprika

3 tbsp (45 ml) sour cream

Preheat the oven to 350°F (175°C, gas mark 4). Line a rimmed baking sheet with parchment paper.

Bake the sweet potato for 25 minutes, or until a knife inserted into the center goes through but the potato is slightly undercooked, then remove it from the oven and let it cool. Turn down the oven to 325°F (165°C, gas mark 3).

In a food processor, pulse the cauliflower once or twice, being careful not to overprocess; it needs to be quite coarse. Transfer the cauliflower to a muslin cloth, and squeeze out any excess liquid. Return the cauliflower to the processor. Scrape out the flesh of the sweet potato with a spoon, and add it to the food processor. Pulse the vegetables until the texture is smooth and they form a tacky dough.

Empty the dough into a bowl, then stir in two-thirds of the Parmesan, the garlic powder, herbs, salt and pepper.

In a separate bowl, combine the quinoa flakes and the remaining one-third of the Parmesan. Break off little pieces of the sweet potato cauli dough, and roll them into bite-sized balls. Roll the balls in the flour, and then in the quinoa mixture.

Place the balls on the prepared baking sheet, leaving ½ inch (1.25 cm) of space between them. Bake the cheese bites for 15 minutes, or until the Parmesan and quinoa flakes look slightly golden in color. Halfway through the cooking time, delicately flip them over to ensure they cook evenly.

For serving, stir the paprika into the sour cream, and serve alongside the cheese bites.

Leftovers can be stored in an airtight container for 2 to 3 days.

BAKED PARMESAN TOMATOES

Tomatoes are known for their abundance of the potent antioxidant lycopene. But, did you know they are also known for their umami flavor? Umami is a blissful flavor that naturally occurs in some foods. It's what makes these baked tomatoes an absolute dreamboat snack. Made with roasted garlic and herbs, adding even more vitamins, this is one of the most moreish snacks you can eat. That's OK, because it contains nothing but good, honest ingredients.

Serves 2-4

¼ cup (60 ml) olive oil

3 cloves garlic, 1 minced and 2 cut into quarters, divided

½ tsp dried thyme

½ tsp dried basil

8 beefsteak tomatoes

Salt, to taste

1 cup (100 g) grated Parmesan cheese

5 fresh basil leaves, roughly torn

Preheat the oven to 450°F (230°C, gas mark 8).

In a bowl, combine the olive oil, minced garlic, thyme and basil. Slice the tomatoes in half crosswise, spread them evenly on a large baking sheet and season them with the salt.

Distribute the pieces of garlic between the tomatoes. Drizzle the olive oil mixture over the tomatoes and garlic, and generously cover the tomatoes with the Parmesan.

Roast the tomatoes for 15 to 20 minutes, until the Parmesan is golden. Top with the basil.

PIRI PIRI CORN ON THE COB

Nachos are one of the most popular snacks, but they can elevate your blood sugar levels and don't give much in the way of health benefits. Here's a nutritious swap that uses the same big flavors and is packed with fiber. Piri Piri Corn on the Cob is so easy to make, and you can dress it up with lots of veggies, hummus or guacamole. This is a simple recipe that's a real flavor bomb.

Serves 4

2½ tsp (12 g) cayenne pepper

½ tsp paprika

2½ tbsp (15 g) piri piri seasoning

4 ears of corn, shucked

Salt, to taste

¼ cup (60 g) butter, cut into 8 equal pieces

2 cups (480 ml) sour cream

2 limes, cut into wedges

Cilantro, for garnish

Preheat the oven to 400°F (200°C, gas mark 6).

Mix the cayenne, paprika and piri piri in a small bowl. Cut your corn into halves widthwise. Tear eight separate pieces of foil big enough to fully cover each piece of corn. Sprinkle each corn piece with about ½ teaspoon of your seasoning mixture, as well as salt.

Place the corn into the foil, and top each piece with one piece of the butter. Wrap up your parcels so they're tight and secure, making sure each edge is properly sealed. Bake the corn for 30 to 35 minutes, or until your corn is tender. Remove the foil and finish the corn on a grill pan to give it grill marks, if you wish. Grill at high heat, turning the pieces for even cooking, for a minute or two.

While the corn is cooking, in a bowl mix the sour cream and the remaining seasoning mixture. Serve the corn stacked up, with the sour cream dip on the side or brushed directly onto the corn. Garnish the corn with the lime wedges and cilantro.

SEEDED CRACKERS AND HUMMUS

Texture is such an important part of our diet, and these crackers have so much crunch that they are a delicious pairing for a dip, especially creamy, nutritious hummus. The mixed seeds are the perfect way to get in your healthy omegas and more filling, digestion-supporting fiber. This is a great recipe to use to replace crackers made with white flour.

Serves 2-4

CRACKERS

1 tbsp (15 ml) olive oil, plus more for greasing

1 cup (140 g) mixed seeds, such as sunflower, pumpkin, sesame, chia, cumin, coriander and caraway

½ cup (80 g) flaxseed

1 tbsp (5 g) psyllium husk powder

½ tsp fine sea salt

1 large egg white

1 tsp dried herbs, such as oregano, Italian seasoning, rosemary and tarragon (optional)

5 to 6 tsp (25 to 30 ml) water

HUMMUS

¼ cup (60 ml) lemon juice (more or less to taste)

2 cloves garlic, roughly diced

½ tsp kosher salt, plus more to taste

½ cup (130 g) good-quality tahini

2 tbsp (30 ml) water

1½ cups (250 g) drained and rinsed canned chickpeas

1 tbsp (15 ml) olive oil

For the crackers, preheat the oven to 340°F (170°C, gas mark 4), and line a baking sheet with parchment paper. Lightly grease the paper and a second sheet of parchment with olive oil.

In a large mixing bowl, thoroughly combine the olive oil, seeds, flaxseed, psyllium husk powder, salt, egg white and herbs, if using. Stir in the water, a teaspoon at a time, until the mixture has a thick, paste-like consistency.

Place the mixture on the prepared parchment in the baking sheet. Put the second piece of greased parchment paper on top of the mixture, oil-side down. Roll out your mixture between the two sheets using a rolling pin, until your mixture is even and about 1⁄16 inch (2 mm) thick. Remove the top layer of parchment paper and place the baking sheet in the oven. Cook the crackers for 20 minutes, or until they are light brown and brittle.

While the cracker mix is cooking, make the hummus. Blend the lemon juice, garlic and salt in a high-powered blender until the garlic is fine. Add the tahini, and blend until the mixture is smooth and the tahini is incorporated. Pause the processor, and drizzle in the water. Process again, until the mixture is smooth, thick and creamy—you may need to add more water, depending on how thick your tahini is.

Add the chickpeas and steadily drizzle in the olive oil, while blending, until the mixture reaches your desired texture—again, add more water, if necessary. Taste the hummus and season it accordingly with lemon juice and salt.

Once the cracker sheet is cool to the touch, break it into shards, putting any that are undercooked back into the oven until they're bone dry. Serve alongside your hummus dip.

TIP

You can add variations to the hummus along with the chickpeas. I love adding some roughly chopped cooked beets or avocado, and I garnish the hummus with an extra drizzle of olive oil or roughly chopped parsley.

GARLIC AND ALMOND BROCCOLINI

This may not jump out as your most crave-worthy snack, but try it. Engage in the mindset that snacks don't equal junk food. Snacks should be a little something you fancy to tide you over between meals. This snack is drenched in that umami flavor, which helps promote meal satiety, keeps you feeling fuller for longer and reduces cravings. Chromium-rich broccolini has a lovely crunch. This snack can be eaten hot or cold; it's packed with minerals, vitamins and fiber.

Serves 2-4

1½ tbsp (23 g) butter

1 medium clove garlic, sliced

15 oz (420 g) broccolini, separated into florets

1 tsp soy sauce or liquid aminos

Handful of toasted sliced almonds

Heat a large frying pan over medium-high heat, then add the butter and melt it. Add the garlic and broccolini to the pan. Cover the pan and cook the broccolini for around 4 minutes, until it's a little soft but still has bite and its vibrant green color. Flip the broccolini occasionally; you may need to reduce the heat.

Remove the lid, and boil off any water in the pan. Add your soy sauce and some of the almonds, and toss the ingredients together. Remove the broccolini from the heat after 2 minutes, or until it begins to slightly char. Sprinkle it with more of the almonds, and serve it immediately.

PARMESAN AND ROSEMARY OATCAKES

It's the small things that can trip you up on any type of diet—it could be as simple as craving something with a bit of crunch, like a cracker, toast or potato chips. None of those things scream health, and that's before you think about what they're topped with or dunked in. Cue these oatcakes to the rescue. Aside from being utterly delicious, oats are great for the nervous system, contain magnesium and can help lower bad cholesterol and regulate blood sugar levels. Rosemary is known for its cognitive and energizing properties and is thought to lower blood insulin; it gives a wonderfully subtle and refreshing flavor. Adding Parmesan creates a stunningly palatable cracker.

Serves 4

2 cups (200 g) rolled oats

1 cup (100 g) porridge oats

½ tsp dried rosemary, very finely crushed

1 tbsp (7 g) grated Parmesan

½ tsp salt

½ cup (120 g) butter, softened

½ cup (120 ml) hot water

1 tbsp (8 g) buckwheat flour

To a large mixing bowl, add the rolled oats, porridge oats, rosemary, Parmesan and salt. In a separate bowl, add the butter and pour in the hot water to create an oily liquid. Then, stir the mixture in with the oats.

Scrape down the edges of the bowl and make sure the mixture is well combined—it should now be a slightly crumbly dough. Ball up the dough, wrap it in plastic wrap and place it in the fridge for 20 to 30 minutes.

Preheat the oven to 350°F (175°C, gas mark 4).

Dust your work surface with the buckwheat flour and roll out the chilled dough with a rolling pin into a wide circle until it's approximately ¹⁄₁₆ inch (2 mm) thick. Using a 3-inch (7-cm) cookie cutter, cut out the oatcakes. Roll the leftover dough back into a dough ball, and repeat the process. Aim for a thin oat cake; you may have to use a spatula to remove them from the surface.

Place the oatcakes on a baking sheet, and cook them for 20 minutes, or until they are crisp, but still have a little give. Transfer the oatcakes to a wire rack to cool them before eating. The oatcakes will keep for 3 days in an airtight container.

SWEET CORN, ZUCCHINI AND FETA FRITTERS

Fritters are a great way to fill up on fresh or canned veggies. These are gluten-free and use high-protein chickpea and buckwheat flours in place of commonly used white flour, which spikes blood sugar. Including feta gives an added boost of filling protein to the fritters. These are easy to make in advance, and they'll keep for a couple of days, stored in the fridge in an airtight container. I jazz them up with a tangy side of Piri Mayo.

Serves 4

FRITTERS

1 lb (455 g) zucchini, grated

1 (7-oz [200-g]) can sweet corn, drained

¾ cup (100 g) chickpea flour (besan)

¼ cup (30 g) buckwheat flour

4 scallions, finely chopped

1 tsp piri piri seasoning

1 tbsp (6 g) chopped fresh mint

1 tbsp (1 g) chopped fresh cilantro

4 oz (115 g) feta cheese, crumbled

2 large eggs, beaten

Salt and pepper, to taste

2 tbsp (30 ml) oil, divided

PIRI MAYO

2 tbsp (30 ml) mayo

1 tsp piri piri seasoning

1 tsp lime juice

FOR SERVING

Salt and pepper, to taste

Fresh mint leaves, torn

Fresh cilantro, torn

Lime wedges

For the fritters, preheat the oven to 300°F (150°C, gas mark 2).

Wrap the zucchini in muslin cloth or paper towels to drain off as much liquid as possible. Pat dry the sweet corn, and crush the kernels so they're flattened.

In a mixing bowl, thoroughly combine the chickpea flour, buckwheat flour, scallions, piri piri seasoning, mint, cilantro, feta, eggs and salt and pepper. Stir in the zucchini and corn, and mix the ingredients together to form a batter.

Heat one-quarter of the oil in a frying pan over medium to low heat for the first round of fritters. Use a large tablespoon to spoon the mixture into the pan. Aim to cook five fritters per round; the batter makes approximately twenty. When you spoon out the mixture, use a spatula to flatten each fritter as it cooks—it should take 3 to 4 minutes to brown, then flip it over and cook the other side. Remove the fritters from the pan, and pop them in the oven to keep them warm while you cook the rest. Repeat, adding one-quarter of the oil to start, for three additional rounds of frying.

To make the Piri Mayo, in a small bowl, stir together the mayonnaise, piri piri seasoning and lime juice.

For serving, plate the fritters, sprinkle with salt and pepper to taste and garnish them with the mint, cilantro and lime wedges. Serve the Piri Mayo on the side.

OMEGA BREAD

Bread can have a similar effect on blood sugar as eating sugar, but it's such a staple in our diet that it can be difficult to completely eliminate. This nutritious recipe is a high-protein swap for other breads, and it will undoubtedly become one of your most-made recipes! With this recipe, you can enjoy bread buttered, toasted and topped.

Serves 4

2 cups (200 g) finely ground almond flour

½ cup (64 g) arrowroot powder

1½ tbsp (15 g) flaxseed

1 tbsp (10 g) chia seeds

½ cup (70 g) mixed seeds, such as pumpkin or sunflower, divided

1 tsp baking soda

½ tsp sea salt

5 large eggs

¼ cup (60 ml) olive oil

1 tbsp (15 ml) apple cider vinegar

Preheat the oven to 350°F (175°C, gas mark 4). Line an 8 x 4–inch (20 x 10–cm) loaf pan with parchment paper.

In a stand mixer, combine the almond flour, arrowroot, flaxseed, chia seeds, three-quarters of the mixed seeds, baking soda and salt and mix on medium speed. Separately, beat the eggs, oil and vinegar together in a bowl, then add the mixture to the dry ingredients, and mix until the ingredients are well combined. Pour the mixture into the loaf pan, and top the batter with the remaining one-fourth of the seeds; ensure the surface is relatively level.

Bake the bread for 30 to 35 minutes, or until it's golden brown and a skewer inserted into the center of the bread comes out clean. Turn the bread onto a wire rack and let it cool.

PICKLED EGGS 3 WAYS

A great source of omega-3 and a high-protein snack, eggs are a trove of vitamins and nutrients. By this stage, you've probably tried eating them every which way . . . but have you tried pickled? This just takes eggs to a whole new taste level. They make the perfect grab-and-go snack, or are great to eat, sliced, on Omega Bread (page 98) or mashed onto the Seeded Crackers (page 90). You can have a lot of fun pickling your eggs in all sorts of aromatics—I've listed my favorites below!

8 large eggs

TRADITIONAL PICKLED EGGS

1 cup (240 ml) water

¾ cup (180 ml) apple cider vinegar

¼ onion, thinly sliced

1 clove garlic

2 bay leaves

1 tsp mustard seeds

1 tsp salt

BEET PICKLED EGGS

1 cup (240 ml) water

¾ cup (180 ml) apple cider vinegar

¼ onion, thinly sliced

2 whole cooked beets, cut into little cubes

2 bay leaves

1 tsp fennel seeds

1 tsp salt

CURRIED PICKLED EGGS

1 cup (240 ml) water

¾ cup (180 ml) apple cider vinegar

¼ onion, thinly sliced

1 clove garlic

1 tbsp (6 g) mild curry powder

1 tsp cumin seeds

1 tsp coriander seeds

1 tsp mustard seeds

1 tsp salt

For the eggs, fill a large bowl with water and ice.

In a large pot, add enough water to cover the eggs by about ½ inch (1.3 cm). Bring the water up to boiling, reduce the heat to medium, and simmer the eggs for 7 minutes. Transfer the eggs to the cold-water bath to cool them. When they are cool, crack the eggs on a hard surface, then peel them in the water to help remove all of the shell.

For the Traditional Pickled Eggs, in a separate pot, bring the water, vinegar, onion, garlic, bay leaves, mustard seeds and salt to a boil, and boil the mixture for 5 minutes. Cool the pickling mixture completely.

For the Beet Pickled Eggs, bring the water, vinegar, onion, beets, bay leaves, fennel seeds and salt to a boil, and boil the mixture for 5 minutes. Cool the pickling mixture completely.

For the Curried Pickled Eggs, bring the water, vinegar, onion, garlic, curry powder, cumin, coriander, mustard seeds and salt to a boil, and boil the mixture for 5 minutes. Cool the pickling mixture completely.

Place the hard-boiled eggs in a large mason jar, and cover them with the pickling mixture of your choice. Seal the jar, and let it rest in the refrigerator for at least 2 days. The pickled eggs keep for 2 weeks.

After the Cleanse
LIVING A LOW- OR NO-SUGAR LIFESTYLE

Congratulations on finishing the 7-day cleanse! You have taken control of your eating habits, are no longer plagued by constant sugar cravings and have broken the sugar addiction cycle.

This last week will also have turned you onto other flavor profiles that are usually masked by added sugars and that make food much more interesting. You have learned more about your eating habits and will now be able to recognize the triggers that lead you to sugar cravings. Most of all though, you have taken the enormous step to improve your quality of life and overall health. Be proud of yourself!

LUNCH AND DINNER *Recipes*

Once you finish the 7-day cleanse, you will have given your body the reset it needs to stop your sugar cravings and break the cycle of sugar addiction. While this doesn't mean you should never eat anything sweet again, it should allow you to make your eating decisions based on your own food choices, and not choices driven by urges and cravings for sugar.

The following lunch and dinner meals are healthy, nutritious recipes that you can make for yourself and your family without worrying about spiking your blood sugar. These are great meals that follow the principles outlined at the start of the book and that are designed to avoid unnatural glucose highs, while keeping you feeling full. They offer you more variety and choice, and they show you the flexibility you can still have living a low- or no-sugar lifestyle.

CHICKEN AND CHORIZO STEW

A stunning and easy high-protein dish, this will keep the hunger hormone ghrelin at bay. The addition of cannellini beans creates texture and gives a mineral boost, which is great because a deficiency in minerals, especially low iron and magnesium, can lead specifically to sugar cravings. Eating a high-sugar diet affects our mineral absorption, so, chances are that you'll need to redouble your intake after the cleanse.

Serves 4

1 tbsp (15 ml) olive oil

2 lbs (900 g) bone-in chicken thighs, with skin

5 oz (150 g) chorizo, chopped

2 onions, chopped

2 cups (128 g) chopped fresh parsley

1⅓ cups (21 g) chopped fresh cilantro

5 cloves garlic, chopped

2 bay leaves

1 tbsp (7 g) smoked paprika

1½ cups (150 g) chopped celery

1 red bell pepper, chopped

4½ cups (800 g) drained and rinsed canned cannellini beans

Pinch of sea salt

¼ cup (35 g) green olives

2 cups (480 ml) chicken or vegetable stock

Heat the oil over high heat in a large, heavy-bottomed frying pan or stewpot. Add the chicken and fry it until the skin browns and crisps, which can take anywhere from 5 minutes to 10, depending on how fatty the meat is. Remove the browned chicken from the pan and set it aside; leave all the fats and juices in the pan to help flavor the stew.

Add the chorizo to the pan. When the fat starts releasing from the chorizo, after 2 to 3 minutes, add the onions and sauté them over medium heat for 5 minutes, until they turn translucent and have absorbed all the gorgeous chicken and chorizo flavors. Add the parsley, cilantro, garlic, bay leaves and paprika, and cook them for 2 minutes. Next, add the celery and bell pepper. Stir in the beans so they can soak up all the rich flavors, and season the stew with a good pinch of salt.

Return the chicken to the pan; add the olives and stock. Cover the pan and cook the stew over medium heat for 1 hour and 30 minutes. Remove the bay leaves, and serve the stew warm.

NOTE

Chicken and Chorizo Stew tastes even better the next day, if you have any leftovers.

VEGGIE SOUP WITH COCONUT "FACON"

This is a great plant-based meal that can be easily adapted for meat lovers by swapping out the "facon"—aka fake bacon—for bacon or torn ham. Thick, creamy and remarkably filling, parsnips are known for their anti-inflammatory and digestive health properties. When we rid our diet of sugar, it gives our bodies a chance to eliminate the buildup of toxins, so it's important to eat foods like antioxidant-rich parsnips that can support this digestive process.

SOUP

1 tsp coconut oil

2 medium onions, chopped

1 medium leek, chopped

½ tsp cumin

6 cloves garlic, minced

4½ cups (600 g) chopped parsnips

2 cups (480 ml) vegetable stock

1 cup (240 ml) coconut milk

Pinch of sea salt

COCONUT "FACON"

1 tsp coconut oil

1 tsp smoked paprika

2 tbsp (30 ml) tamarind sauce

⅓ cup (30 g) unsweetened coconut flakes

Preheat the oven to 350°F (175°C, gas mark 4).

For the soup, heat the oil in a saucepan over low to medium heat, add the onions and the leek, and sauté for 4 minutes, until the vegetables are slightly browned. Sprinkle in the cumin and stir it into the onions, then add the garlic. Cook the mixture for 3 minutes, or until the cumin starts to catch a little on the base of the pan, then add in the parsnips and the stock. Boil the soup for 10 minutes, until the parsnips soften, then reduce the heat to a simmer and add the coconut milk and salt.

While the soup simmers, make the Coconut "Facon." In a medium bowl, mix together the oil, paprika and tamarind until they form a paste. Then, add the coconut flakes and toss until they get evenly covered.

Spread the coated coconut flakes on a baking sheet, making sure the flakes are spaced out, and bake them for 15 minutes, or until they are crisp. Check after 5 minutes, and give the pan a little shake, so the flakes turn over. The aim is for these coconut flakes to be lovely, crispy bursts of smoky flavor.

Return to making the soup while the facon cooks. Using an immersion blender, blend the soup until it's smooth and creamy. Ladle the soup into four bowls, and scatter a handful of the facon into each bowl.

SWEET POTATO AND SPINACH TORTILLA

Sweet potatoes are a great source of chromium, the mineral known to help reduce sugar cravings and regulate blood sugar levels. Sweet potatoes also have a low glycemic index, and they add a whole new dynamic to tortillas. This is a great post-detox dish, because it's a perfect high-protein evening meal for when you are short on time or fatigued from your day and hungry. It's great to eat cold the next day, too.

Serves 4

TORTILLA

¼ cup (60 ml) olive oil, divided

2 large onions, thinly sliced

2 cloves garlic, minced

4 medium sweet potatoes, thinly sliced

Pinch of salt and pepper

8 large eggs

10 cups (300 g) spinach leaves

1 tsp freshly grated nutmeg

FOR SERVING

Smoked salmon and horseradish or hot sauce and mayonnaise (optional)

In a nonstick frying pan with a lid, heat 2 tablespoons (30 ml) of the oil over low to medium heat, then add the onions. Cook the onions for 5 minutes, until they're translucent and soft, then add the garlic and cook it for 1 minute; add the potatoes. Season the mixture with the salt and pepper, cover the pan and cook the potatoes over low heat for 10 to 15 minutes, or until the potatoes are softened.

In a mixing bowl, whisk the eggs then transfer the onion and potato mixture from the frying pan to the mixing bowl. Gently stir them through the eggs, being careful to keep the potato slices whole. Add the spinach and nutmeg. Heat the remaining 2 tablespoons (30 ml) of oil in the frying pan, and pour in the egg and potato mixture.

Add the lid to the pan, and cook the tortilla over gentle heat for 20 minutes. It is important to keep it on a low heat, so that it cooks through fully without burning. Using a plate placed over the pan, carefully flip the tortilla over and slide it back into the pan for a few minutes, until a knife inserted into the tortilla comes out clean and the other side is slightly browned.

When it's ready to serve, cut the tortilla into eight slices in the pan. Remove them with a spatula or, using the same method as flipping it, place a plate over the pan and turn it out. For serving, add optional toppings like smoked salmon and horseradish or hot sauce and mayonnaise.

ORANGE AND FENNEL ROASTED CHICKEN

This is a wonderfully aromatic dinner that soothes. Restorative fennel is refreshing and warming, and it pairs wonderfully with calming sweet oranges. After a week free from refined sugar, the orange will really sing through this dish, which is a delicious take on the traditional roast chicken. I like to serve this with quinoa, cauli rice or brown rice. Be sure to spoon the sauce over the chicken.

Serves 4

3 tbsp (45 ml) olive oil

15 oz (420 g) bone-in chicken thighs, with skin scored

1 medium onion, finely sliced into rings

4 cloves garlic, minced

¾ cup (20 g) chopped parsley

1 tbsp (15 g) whole-grain mustard

2 fennel bulbs, sliced

2 oranges, 1 sliced and 1 juiced

1 cup (240 ml) chicken stock

1 tsp salt

1 tsp pepper

Preheat the oven to 370°F (185°C, gas mark 5).

Heat the oil over high heat in an ovenproof heavy-bottomed frying pan. Cook the chicken thighs on both sides for a few minutes, until they start to brown. Remove the thighs from the pan and set them aside.

Reduce the heat to medium, and sauté the onion for 5 minutes, until it is translucent. Stir in the garlic, parsley and mustard, and cook them for a few minutes.

Add the fennel, and cook it for 2 minutes, or until it releases its aromatic flavor. At that point, add the orange slices and orange juice. Cook the mixture over low to medium heat for 3 to 5 minutes, until the liquid is reduced and the sauce slightly thickened.

Return the chicken to the pan. Using tongs, rub each thigh in the sauce, then spoon the mixture over the scored skin—this helps the flavor penetrate the meat better. Then pour in the chicken stock and sprinkle the mixture with the salt and pepper. Bake the chicken for 25 minutes, or until there is no sign of redness when you cut into the thickest part of a piece.

BETTER-FOR-YOU LAMB BURGERS ON FLATBREAD WITH SUMAC YOGURT

This recipe proves that your lifestyle post–sugar cleanse can still be full of favorite meals and more. With global burger chains reigning supreme in the world of fast food, it's clearly a meal beloved by our nations. Far be it from me to deprive you of the burger, so here's a culinary beauty that will satiate the biggest of Elvis-burger appetites. The sugary condiments are gone, in favor of a gut-loving mint yogurt.

Serves 4

FLATBREAD

½ cup (120 ml) plain full-fat Greek yogurt

½ cup (64 g) arrowroot powder

½ cup (50 g) finely ground almond flour

1 tbsp (15 ml) olive oil

Pinch of salt

1 tsp coconut oil

BURGERS

1 tbsp (15 ml) coconut or olive oil, divided

1 medium red onion, finely chopped

21 oz (600 g) ground lamb

2¾ cups (264 g) chopped fresh mint

1 tbsp (8 g) garlic powder

½ tsp chili flakes (optional)

1 tbsp (18 g) salt, plus a pinch

⅓ cup (80 ml) plain full-fat Greek yogurt

1 tbsp (6 g) sumac

Juice of half a lemon

5 cups (100 g) arugula

To make the flatbread, preheat the oven to 325°F (165°C, gas mark 3).

Stir together the yogurt, arrowroot, almond flour, olive oil and salt to make a batter. The batter will appear a little stodgy; this is the correct consistency.

Heat the coconut oil over low heat in a frying pan. Spoon one-quarter of the batter into the pan, and use the back of the spoon to gently smooth out the batter and shape it into an approximately 5-inch (13-cm) circle. Cook the first side for 4 minutes, or until the edges of the bread start to crisp slightly, then flip it. Be patient; if you flip the bread too soon, it will break. Cook the second side for 4 minutes, until the edges have crisped. Pop the flatbread into the oven to keep it warm. Spoon out another portion, and repeat the process to cook the remaining three flatbreads.

Then, to make the burgers, heat half of the oil over low to medium heat in a frying pan, then fry the onion for 5 minutes, until softened; remove it from the heat and let it cool a little.

In a mixing bowl, mix the lamb, mint, garlic powder, chili flakes, if using, salt and the cooled onion until the lamb is broken down and the ingredients are well combined. Shape the mixture to make four patties or eight mini ones.

In the same pan you used for the onion, heat the remaining half of the oil and pop in the burgers. Cook them over low heat for 6 minutes on each side; cook them a little longer if you like the meat well done. The burgers should be nice and brown on the outside and cooked all the way through inside with an even color.

In a medium bowl, whisk together the yogurt, sumac, lemon juice and pinch of salt.

When the lamb burgers are cooked to your liking, remove them from the pan, and pop them on top of the flatbreads with the arugula and yogurt dip.

SWEET AND SOUR SALMON WITH WILD RICE

Salmon is one of the healthiest types of fish we can eat. It's filled with heart-healthy fats and omega-3s. Eating foods rich in omega-3 is so important to rebuild our wellness after coming off a sugar-heavy diet. The sweet and sour ingredients used in this recipe make this a divine evening meal option; it's filling without being too heavy.

¾ cup (150 g) wild rice

Pinch of salt, plus more as needed

2 tbsp (30 ml) oil

2½ cups (40 g) roughly chopped fresh cilantro, divided

½-inch (1.3-cm) piece of ginger, finely grated

2 cloves garlic, minced

2 star anise

1 tbsp (15 ml) fish sauce

2 tbsp (30 ml) rice wine, white wine or apple cider vinegar

17 oz (480 g) fresh or thawed frozen salmon fillets

1 red bell pepper, julienned

¾ cup (112 g) cherry tomatoes, halved

6 scallions, julienned

1 red chile pepper, thinly sliced

1 mango, diced

Juice of half a lime

Preheat the oven to 350°F (175°C, gas mark 4).

Cook the rice as directed on the package, adding the salt.

Mix the oil, half of the cilantro, the ginger, garlic, star anise, fish sauce and vinegar in a cup until well combined. Place the fish fillets in a baking dish and pour the oil mixture over them. Top that with the bell pepper, tomatoes, scallions, chile and mango. Season the vegetables and fruit with salt.

Cover the pan with foil and bake the fish for 20 minutes, or until the salmon has an even pink color all the way through.

When the rice is cooked, drain it, and stir in the remaining half of the cilantro and the lime juice.

Remove the salmon from the oven when it has finished cooking, plate up the rice and add the salmon and the veggies. If there are juices left in the baking dish, drizzle them over the veggies.

IRISH HAM AND CABBAGE ONE-POT WITH PARSLEY SAUCE

Post-cleanse, it's important to have a bunch of nutritious go-to recipes that are dependable, easy and delicious. *Bagún agus cabáiste*—bacon and cabbage—was a staple in my Irish home growing up. My dad would make it because it was a simple, tasty dinner. This stalwart of a healthy one-pot wonder is brimming with goodness. The cabbage aids digestion and helps support the colon and digestive tract. Reserve the stock in the pot; drinking it soothes the stomach.

PORK

2¼ lbs (1 kg) pork loin

2 onions, halved widthwise

8 cloves

2 carrots, chopped into big chunks

3 ribs celery, cut into 1-inch (2.5-cm) pieces

Sprig of fresh thyme and parsley

1 head of cabbage, chopped

½ tsp white pepper

PARSLEY SAUCE

⅔ cup (160 ml) stock, from the pork

⅔ cup (160 ml) heavy cream

3 tbsp (54 g) English mustard

1 cup (30 g) chopped fresh parsley

Fill a large saucepan with cold water, add the pork loin and bring the water to a boil, skimming any white foam that comes to the surface.

Pierce each onion half with two cloves, then add them to the pork stock along with the carrots, celery, thyme and parsley. Simmer the pot, covered, for 1 hour.

Remove the clove onions, thyme and parsley, leaving just the carrots, stock and the pork loin—the celery will mostly have dissolved. Stir in the cabbage and white pepper, and simmer the mixture for 30 minutes.

For the Parsley Sauce, with a ladle, remove ⅔ cup (160 ml) of the stock from the meat pot. In a small saucepan over low to medium heat, whisk together the stock, cream, mustard and parsley for about 4 to 5 minutes, until the sauce has a runny, creamy consistency.

Transfer the pork from the saucepan to a chopping board, then cut it into slices; spoon some of the stock from the saucepan over the meat to keep it moist. Using a strainer, transfer the cabbage and carrots from the stock to a serving bowl, then stack the meat on top. Pour the sauce over the meat and serve immediately.

BUTTER CHICKEN WITH CAULIFLOWER RICE

This is an outrageously delicious dinner that you will look forward to time and time again. Butter chicken is wonderfully rich, without being overpowering, and boasts the most beautiful deep flavors. This dinner really shows how easy it is to cook real, nutritious food that doesn't need sugar.

BUTTER CHICKEN

2 lbs (900 g) boneless, skinless chicken breasts, cut into chunks

1 tsp chili powder

½ tsp ground turmeric

6 tbsp (90 g) butter, divided into 3 chunks

2 onions, finely chopped

3 cloves garlic, crushed

1-inch (2.5-cm) piece of ginger, grated

2 tbsp (16 g) cinnamon

1 tbsp (6 g) garam masala

1 tsp cumin

1 tsp cayenne pepper

1 tsp salt, plus more to taste

1 tsp pepper

18 oz (500 g) passata or canned tomatoes

1 cup (240 ml) water

1 cup (240 ml) heavy cream

CAULIFLOWER RICE

1 medium cauliflower, roughly chopped

1 medium carrot, roughly chopped

1 bunch scallions, roughly chopped

Salt, to taste

1 cup (30 g) roughly chopped fresh parsley

1 clove garlic, roughly chopped

1½ tbsp (23 ml) olive oil

For the chicken, mix together the chicken, chili powder and turmeric in a large bowl. Let the meat marinate for 15 minutes.

Melt 2 tablespoons (30 g) of the butter over medium heat in a heavy-bottomed pan, add the chicken and cook it for 10 minutes, or until it's browned. Remove the chicken from the pan and set it aside.

In the same pan, melt another 2 tablespoons (30 g) of the butter and add the onions, garlic, ginger, cinnamon, garam masala, cumin, cayenne, salt and pepper. Sauté the mixture for 3 minutes, until the aromas of the spices are released. Add the passata, and cook the mixture over medium-low heat until it begins to simmer. Stir in the water and cream, then return the chicken to the pot.

Cover the pot and cook the mixture for 10 minutes to let the flavors infuse. Stir in the last 2 tablespoons (30 g) of butter and additional salt.

For the cauliflower rice, use a food processor to blend the cauliflower, carrot, scallions, salt, parsley and garlic until the mixture is the consistency of rice.

Heat the oil over high heat in a frying pan, add the cauliflower rice and spread it out evenly. Cook the rice for 3 to 4 minutes, stirring continuously, until it's golden brown. Alternatively, you can cook the cauliflower rice on a baking sheet for 10 minutes in an oven preheated to 400°F (200°C, gas mark 6).

COWBOY BEANS WITH CHEESY TOAST

This recipe is an inexpensive wellspring of fiber and incredibly easy to make. I've mentioned often the importance of fiber in our diet, but it's equally important to get fiber from multiple sources to really bolster gut health and our microbiome. Fiber is also a key to satiety and fending off sugar cravings, so it'll help you keep living your healthier post-cleanse lifestyle.

Serves 4

COWBOY BEANS

2 tbsp (30 g) butter

2 yellow onions, finely chopped

4 cloves garlic, minced

1 red chile pepper, seeded if you prefer less heat

1 tbsp (7 g) smoked paprika

2 tsp (3 g) cayenne pepper

1 tsp cumin

1 tsp cinnamon

¼ cup (15 g) chopped fresh parsley

¼ cup (4 g) chopped fresh cilantro

2⅓ cups (400 g) drained and rinsed canned kidney beans

2¼ cups (400 g) drained and rinsed canned cannellini beans

2 cups (400 g) drained and rinsed canned butter beans

2⅓ cups (400 g) drained and rinsed canned navy beans

Salt, to taste

32 oz (905 g) passata

1½ cups (360 ml) chicken or vegetable stock

1 tbsp (15 ml) Spicy Tomato Dip (page 78) or sugar-free ketchup

1 tbsp (15 ml) Worcestershire or soy sauce

1–2 tbsp (15–30 ml) milk

CHEESY TOAST

2 tsp (10 g) butter, divided

4 (½-inch [1.3-cm]) slices of Omega Bread (page 98)

2 cups (224 g) grated Monterey Jack cheese, divided

FOR SERVING

Grated cheese

Sour cream

Guacamole (page 55)

For the beans, in a large heavy-bottomed pot, melt the butter over medium heat. Add the onions, garlic, chile, paprika, cayenne, cumin and cinnamon. Sauté the mixture for 5 minutes, until the onions are browned. Stir in the parsley and cilantro, and cook the mixture for 1 minute. Stir in the kidney, cannellini, butter and navy beans, and season the pot generously with the salt. Cook the mixture for 2 minutes, continuously stirring.

Next, add the passata and stock, stir well for 1 minute, cover the pot and cook the mixture for 10 minutes. Uncover the pan, and stir in the Spicy Tomato Dip, Worcestershire and milk. Cook the mixture, uncovered, for 10 minutes, stirring occasionally, taking care not to let it come to a boil.

For the Cheesy Toast, preheat the broiler in the oven or a toaster oven to medium. Divide the butter among the slices of bread and spread it. Sprinkle the butter on each slice with one-quarter of the cheese. Broil the toast for 5 minutes, or until the cheese begins to brown and bubble. Serve the toast immediately, with the beans topped with grated cheese, sour cream and guacamole.

SWEET POTATO GNOCCHI WITH PESTO

Nothing says comfort food more than the pillowy delight that is gnocchi, so this was an essential recipe to be included in this cookbook. Living a low- or no-sugar diet isn't about never eating indulgent go-tos again. It's about making small tweaks to ingredients, so you can still have all your favorites, but in a healthier way!

GNOCCHI

1 large sweet potato

Salt, to taste

2½ cups (250 g) finely ground almond flour, plus more for dusting

1 cup (128 g) arrowroot powder

1 large egg

PESTO OIL

¼ cup (34 g) pine nuts, plus a few for garnish (optional)

1¾ cups (42 g) fresh basil leaves, plus a few for garnish

2 cloves garlic, grated

⅓ cup (33 g) grated Parmesan cheese, plus a little for the topping

1 tsp lemon zest

1 tbsp (15 ml) lemon juice

Salt, to taste

¼ cup (60 ml) olive oil

For the gnocchi, preheat the oven to 425°F (220°C, gas mark 7) and line a baking sheet with parchment paper.

Poke the sweet potato a few times with the tines of a fork, and bake it on the baking sheet for 45 to 50 minutes, or until a knife inserted into the center slides in easily. Let the sweet potato cool, then remove the skin.

Make the pesto while the sweet potato is baking. In a pan, toast the pine nuts over medium heat for 1 minute, or until they are golden brown, being sure to shake the pan to brown them evenly. In a blender, blend the pine nuts, basil, garlic, Parmesan, lemon zest and juice and salt until it's a rough paste. Slowly and steadily add the olive oil while the blender is on, if the lid allows. If not, pause the blender, remove the lid and add a little oil at a time, blend and repeat until you have the desired consistency. Refrigerate the pesto while you make the gnocchi.

Using a ricer or potato masher, mash the sweet potato in a big bowl, and season it generously with the salt. Let it sit longer if it's still a little warm. Next, add the flour, arrowroot and the egg to the sweet potato. Mix together until all of the ingredients are fully incorporated.

On a clean, flat surface dusted with almond flour, divide the mixture into sections and roll them out into a 1-inch (2.5-cm)-thick long tube, then slice the tube into 1-inch (2.5-cm) pieces. To give your gnocchi some character, gently roll a fork onto the pieces, creating those signature indentations.

Bring a large pot of heavily salted water to a boil. Add the gnocchi batch by batch, roughly 8 to 10 at a time, depending on the size of your pan. There should be at least an inch (2.5 cm) around each gnocchi and you should allow 2 to 3 minutes of cooking time; the gnocchi are done when they float to the top. Use a slotted spoon to remove the gnocchi, when cooked.

Serve the gnocchi, tossed in the pesto and topped with the reserved pine nuts, if using, basil and Parmesan.

DESSERT *Recipes*

The question I get asked most after readers complete my sugar-free program is, "Can I ever eat sugar again?" My answer is always the same, "Yes, you can, but you just won't have those same intense cravings." The less you eat, the less you crave, and the smallest bit goes a long way.

The point is, now that you've broken your sugar cycle, you'll no longer need the excessively sweetened flavors of processed sweets. You begin to really taste again. So, when you do want something sweet, you'll find that just a little in a healthier, better way is more than enough to satisfy you.

That's why, in this chapter, I've provided naturally sweetened desserts that offer a healthy and delicious twist on your former traditional sugary favorites. Eating sugar in moderation isn't actually harmful; it's when we eat too much that it becomes an issue. This cleanse is designed to ensure that you break away from urges and cravings that drive you to eat too much sugar. Once you are back in control of your sugar consumption, eating small portions of naturally sweetened foods is fine—it's all about us being in control of our eating rather than the other way around.

Because I've sweetened these recipes with real food ingredients that contain fiber and other nutrients, your body registers the full feeling, unlike with processed sugar that bypasses the satiety hormone, leptin. These dessert recipes offer a healthy and delicious twist on the traditional sugary favorites, so you can still "have your cake and eat it too."

SALTED CARAMEL PECAN NICE CREAM

We see ice cream being used in films all the time as a bit of an emotional crutch. It's synonymous with helping people get through the tough times. But, take a cursory glance at the back of an ice cream tub and you'll see it's no hero. Sugar is often the most prominent ingredient. My focus is on making healthy re-creations, and this "nice cream" is a great example of healthy being delicious. Enjoy this thick, creamy nice cream with a date caramel flavor that is loaded with nutrients and is vegan-friendly, too.

Serves 8

2 tbsp (30 g) salted butter

4 ripe bananas, cut into 1-inch (2.5-cm)-thick pieces, divided

¼ cup (40 g) pitted dried Medjool dates

¾ cup (180 ml) coconut cream

¾ cup (80 g) roughly chopped toasted pecans

A day ahead of making this ice cream, you will need to caramelize half of the bananas, and then pop all of the slices into the freezer overnight.

To caramelize the bananas, melt the butter over medium to high heat in a frying pan, then add half of the slices. Cook them for 1 to 2 minutes, until they start to brown and stick a little to the pan, then turn the slices over to brown the other side. When they are nicely golden, transfer the caramelized bananas and any caramelized buttery bits sticking to the pan to an airtight container and freeze them overnight. Also, freeze the remaining plain banana slices overnight in a resealable plastic bag or airtight container.

When you're ready to start making the ice cream, put the dates in a bowl, add enough boiled water to submerge them and let them soak for 10 minutes. Then, drain the water, reserving 2 tablespoons (30 ml). Put the reserved water and dates into a food processor, and process until the ingredients become a slightly runny, smooth paste; let the mixture cool.

When the date paste is cool, make the nice cream. Add all of the frozen banana slices to the food processor with the date paste. Process until the bananas start to break down and combine with the dates. Through the feed tube, slowly start adding the coconut cream, little by little, until it's incorporated. The mixture should have a nice, thick ice cream consistency. Empty the nice cream mixture into a container, and fold in the pecans.

Freeze the nice cream for at least 30 minutes, or up to a couple of days if you want to make it in advance. For advance prep, remove the nice cream from the freezer for 10 to 15 minutes to soften it before serving.

TURKISH DELIGHT CHIA PUDDING

It is the rose in Turkish delight candy that gives it that distinctive flavor, and it's all the insulin-spiking sugar, inverted syrup, high-fructose corn syrup and powdered sugar that makes it so nauseating when you've eaten one too many. Instead of the sugar-laden nasties, this recipe returns rose to the center of the show and celebrates its stunning, subtle flavor in this protein-packed, no-added-sugar treat. Rose is also known for its calming and restorative properties.

Serves 4

½ cup (60 g) raspberries, pureed and pressed through a sieve to remove the seeds

8 tbsp (80 g) chia seeds

1 tbsp (15 ml) vanilla extract

2 tbsp (30 ml) rose water

1 cup (240 ml) coconut milk

¼ cup (60 ml) coconut cream

2 tbsp (14 g) chopped pistachio nuts, divided

2 tbsp (8 g) edible dried rose petals, divided

In a large bowl, stir together the pureed raspberries, chia seeds, vanilla, rose water and coconut milk until they're completely combined. Refrigerate the mixture for 10 minutes, then stir it again to stop the chia from clumping. Return the mixture to the fridge for 30 minutes to 1 hour, until it has thickened to the consistency of rice pudding.

Using a whisk, whip the coconut cream for a minute or so, until it thickens.

Remove the chia mix from the fridge, spoon it into four bowls and top each serving with a tablespoon (15 ml) of the whipped coconut cream and one-quarter of the pistachios and rose petals.

WHIPPED RASPBERRY AND GINGER CHEESECAKE

This is an absolute taste revelation and the most delicious way to guide you away from refined sugar. It's a pot of sweet, velvety, spiced splendor that builds with every single mouthful. Sugar-free life doesn't get much sweeter than this.

Serves 4

½ cup (50 g) rolled oats

⅓ cup (50 g) hazelnuts or almonds, or a mix of both

⅓ cup (50 g) pitted dried Medjool dates

1 tbsp (8 g) cinnamon

1 tbsp (8 g) ground cardamon (optional)

1 tbsp (15 g) unsalted butter

1 tbsp (15 g) vanilla bean paste

¾ cup (100 g) raspberries, divided, plus more for garnish

1½ tbsp (8 g) ground ginger

1½ cups (300 g) mascarpone or cream cheese

Sliced almonds, to garnish

In a blender, blend the oats, hazelnuts and almonds, dates, cinnamon, cardamom, if using, butter and vanilla paste until it forms a tacky mixture that clumps easily together. Spoon out the mixture into four 6-oz (180-ml) ramekins to form a thick base, pressing the mixture with the back of the spoon to compact it.

For the cheesecake filling, puree ½ cup (66 g) of the raspberries in a blender, then press them through a sieve to catch any seeds. In a large mixing bowl, whisk together the seedless puree, ginger and mascarpone, until the ingredients are fully combined and have a lovely fluffy texture.

Spoon the filling on top of the base in the ramekins, and garnish each serving with the reserved raspberries and almonds. Refrigerate the ramekins for 30 minutes, then serve.

FANCY CHOCOLATE TORTE

Craving chocolate can sometimes be a sign of possible magnesium deficiency. This delicious chocolate torte is made with no added sugar and cacao, which can be found in dark chocolate and is antioxidant-rich and a great source of magnesium. With this recipe, you really can have your cake and eat it, too!

Serves 6

1¼ cups (200 g) pitted dried prunes

⅓ cup (80 ml) sugar-free grape juice

2 tbsp (30 g) vanilla bean paste

2 tbsp (30 ml) oil (I use olive)

½ cup (120 ml) water

3 large eggs, beaten

1½ cups (150 g) finely ground almond flour

¼ cup (25 g) cacao powder

¼ cup (25 g) unsweetened cocoa powder

½ tsp baking powder

Pinch of salt

Preheat the oven to 325°F (165°C, gas mark 3), and grease a 9-inch (23-cm) cake pan, ideally a springform.

In a saucepan, simmer the prunes and grape juice over medium heat for 3 to 5 minutes, until the liquid has reduced to roughly 2 tablespoons (30 ml). Then, remove the pan from the heat and let the mixture cool. In a blender, blend the cooled prune mixture, vanilla, oil and water until the mixture forms a smooth paste. Transfer the mixture to a large mixing bowl and stir in the eggs, until they are well-incorporated.

In a separate mixing bowl, combine the almond flour, cacao powder, cocoa powder, baking powder and salt. Transfer the flour mixture to the prune mixture, and stir until the batter is smooth. Pour the batter into the cake pan, and bake the cake for 25 minutes, or until a knife inserted into the center of the cake comes out clean. Remove the band from the pan, and let the cake cool a little. This cake is best served warm, with an optional whipped topping of your choice.

STRAWBERRY AND ALMOND CAKE

This is a delightful cake that is light and airy and pairs so well with a dollop of fresh vanilla cream. The recipe uses almond flour, which stabilizes blood sugar and is also high in protein. This is a great no-added-sugar alternative to the typical birthday cakes that are filled with syrupy jams and covered in sugary icing.

Serves 8

½ cup (80 g) pitted dried Medjool dates

1 very ripe banana

4 large eggs, whites and yolks separated into two bowls

1 tsp vanilla extract

2 cups (200 g) finely ground almond flour

1 tsp baking powder

½ cup (120 g) butter, softened

Pinch of salt

1½ cups (200 g) thickly sliced fresh strawberries

¼ cup (25 g) whipped cream for topping (optional)

Preheat the oven to 325°F (165°C, gas mark 3), and grease a 9-inch (23-cm) round springform pan.

Place the dates in a small bowl, add enough boiled water to submerge them and let them soak for 10 minutes. Drain the dates, reserving 3 tablespoons (45 ml) of the water.

In a blender, blend the dates and banana into a smooth paste. Add the reserved water, a little at a time, if needed, to make the paste smooth; some dates may be softer than others. Then, add the egg yolks and vanilla and blend until frothy.

In a large mixing bowl, mix together the almond flour, baking powder, butter and salt, until they are combined into a fine crumb; I use my hands for this. Then, make a well in the middle of the mixture and stir in the date and egg yolk mixture, little by little, until they are thoroughly combined; the mixture will be somewhere between a wet dough and batter.

Next, whisk the egg whites until stiff peaks form, which happens when you lift up your whisk and you get a nice peak that holds its shape. Then, lightly, bit by bit, fold the egg whites into the dough.

Add the chopped strawberries to the mix and gently fold in. With a spatula, carefully spoon the mixture into the prepared cake pan. Bake the cake for 35 minutes, then insert a toothpick into the center of the cake; if it comes out clean, remove the cake from the oven. If not, return the cake to the oven for 5 or so minutes, until a toothpick comes out clean.

Let the cake cool in the pan, then remove the band from the pan. Serve warm or cold, with the whipped cream, if using.

BOOZY BUBBLY BERRY JELL-O

Sometimes life calls for a little celebration, and this effervescent number is a real party dessert. The Prosecco could be swapped for more apple juice, mixed with sparkling water, for a non-alcoholic version with all the bubbles. This is another example of how desserts do not have to equal sugar! Naturally sweetened with the apple juice and the berries, this is a lovely, refreshing, fun dessert.

Serves 4

6 gelatin leaves or sheets

⅓ cup (80 ml) apple juice

3 cups (720 ml) Prosecco

1 cup (150 g) summer berries, divided

Place the gelatin leaves in a saucepan, cover them with the apple juice and let the mixture sit for 10 minutes. Then, place the pan on the stove and, over low heat, gently warm the mixture for 5 minutes, until the leaves have dissolved into a gooey liquid. Be careful not to let the mixture boil. Remove the mixture from the heat, pour in the Prosecco and gently stir to combine the ingredients.

Pour the gelatin-infused Prosecco into four glasses, and add one-quarter of the summer fruits. Some of the berries will rise to the top. Gently just tap them back down. Refrigerate the dessert for 4 to 5 hours, or longer, if needed, until it is set. Serve chilled.

NOTE

Gelatin leaves can be found in your grocery store. Or, powdered gelatin can be used. Substitute 2½ teaspoons (7 g) of powdered gelatin per two gelatin leaves.

STICKY TOFFEE PUDDING

This is a healthier version, replete with wholesome ingredients, of the classic Sticky Toffee Pudding. Replacing white flour with almond flour helps to stabilize blood sugars, and sweetening the dessert with fiber-rich dates makes this a healthier choice than refined sugar. The fiber makes this more filling, so you're less inclined to eat a big portion!

Serves 8

PUDDING

15 pitted dried Medjool dates

2 large eggs, whites and yolks separated into two bowls

1 tbsp (15 g) vanilla bean paste

½ cup (120 g) butter, softened

1½ cups (150 g) finely ground almond flour

½ cup (60 g) chopped walnuts

1 tsp unsweetened cocoa powder

Pinch of salt

1 tsp baking powder

TOFFEE SAUCE

¼ cup (60 g) butter

6 pitted dried Medjool dates

1 tsp vanilla bean paste

½ cup (120 ml) heavy cream

Preheat the oven to 350°F (175°C, gas mark 4). Grease a 7-inch (18-cm) square cake pan, then line it with parchment paper.

Start with the cake by putting the dates in a bowl. Add enough boiled water to submerge them, and let them soak for 10 minutes. Drain the dates, reserving 2 teaspoons (10 ml) of the water. While the dates soak, beat the egg yolks for 1 minute, until they are frothy and a paler shade of orange. Set aside the egg yolks.

In a blender, blend the dates until a smooth paste forms; add the reserved water and blend again, if needed, to achieve the paste. Then, add the vanilla paste and blend again. Next add the egg yolks and butter, blend the mixture together, scrape down the sides of the blender with a spatula and blend again.

In a large mixing bowl, combine the almond flour, nuts, cocoa powder and salt. Sift in the baking powder, then combine all the ingredients. Slowly add the date and yolk mixture to the flour mixture, stirring well after each addition, until the batter is well combined.

In a separate bowl, whisk the egg whites until they form stiff peaks, which is when you lift up your whisk and you get a nice peak that holds its shape. Gently fold the egg whites into the batter. Be careful to keep as much air in the egg whites as possible by not over-stirring and being gentle—this helps keep the cake light. Pour the batter into the prepared pan and bake the cake for 35 minutes. Check the cake; if a toothpick inserted into the center comes out clean, the cake is done. If needed, bake the cake for 5 minutes more, until the toothpick is clean. When the cake is done, remove it from the oven and let it cool slightly.

For the Toffee Sauce, in a saucepan, melt the butter over medium heat. While that melts, put the dates in a blender with 2 tablespoons (30 ml) of hot water, and blend until the dates are completely smooth. Add the dates to the melted butter. Next, add the vanilla bean paste and keep stirring for 1 minute. Then, turn the heat down to low and start slowly pouring in the cream, stirring as you do—be careful to make sure that the mixture doesn't boil—until all of the cream is incorporated and the sauce is warm.

Slice the cake, drizzle the slices with the sauce and eat immediately.

AFTERNOON TEA ENGLISH MUFFINS WITH PEACHES AND CREAM

You have to have something special for an event to become a tradition. Anyone who's enjoyed afternoon tea knows that the English muffin holds a special place in that tradition. This tweaked recipe of the popular classic is a healthier version that swaps the sugar-spiking ingredients for more insulin-stabilizing ones. Instead of sweet, sticky jam, I've used fresh sliced peaches with a hint of thyme for a stunning alternative.

Serves 4

1½ cups (150 g) finely ground almond flour

¼ cup (28 g) coconut flour

1 tsp baking soda

1 tsp baking powder

4 large eggs, beaten

½ cup (120 ml) buttermilk

1½ tbsp (23 g) vanilla bean paste, divided

¼ cup (20 g) golden raisins (optional)

2 tbsp (30 ml) melted coconut oil

½ tsp finely chopped fresh thyme

2 tbsp (30 ml) heavy cream

½ cup (72 g) sliced peaches

Preheat the oven to 350°F (175°C, gas mark 4). Lightly grease a baking sheet, then line it with parchment paper.

In a large mixing bowl, sift in the almond and coconut flours, baking soda and baking powder. The coconut flour may clump a little, so sift it as best you can.

In a separate bowl, whisk the eggs and the buttermilk together with 1 tablespoon (15 g) of the vanilla paste. Form a well in the center of the flour mixture, and pour in the egg mixture. Bit by bit, fold in the dry ingredients to form a wet dough. Add the raisins, if using, and the coconut oil and combine.

On the parchment paper–lined baking sheet, form four round muffin shapes with the dough and bake them for 10 minutes. Then, flip them over to cook the other side for 5 minutes, or until they are browned.

While the muffins bake, in a bowl, whisk the remaining ½ tablespoon (8 g) vanilla bean paste, thyme and cream until the cream forms soft peaks. When the muffins are cooked, remove them from the oven and let them cool a little.

Serve the muffins with a dollop of the whipped cream, and top them with the peaches.

NOTE

This recipe is easily converted to a savory treat. Just leave out the vanilla and raisins and replace them with 2 tablespoons (30 g) of grated cheese and 1 tablespoon (4 g) of chopped fresh chives. For serving, slather them in butter.

BLACKBERRY JAM TARTS

The jam tarts caused a right ruckus in *Alice in Wonderland*, and, if you've ever eaten one, it's easy to see why. The problem is that jam requires a teeth-rotting amount of sugar. So, here's a refined sugar–free, healthy version fit for a Queen (of Hearts).

Serves 6

CRUST

8 pitted dried Medjool dates

⅓ cup (50 g) golden raisins

⅔ cup (160 ml) hot water, divided

3 cups (300 g) rolled oats

1 tsp cinnamon

1 tbsp (15 g) vanilla bean paste

½ cup (120 g) butter, softened

1 tbsp (8 g) buckwheat flour

JAM

1 cup (150 g) blackberries

1 tbsp (15 ml) tart cherry juice (if unavailable, add another tablespoon [10 g] chia)

2 tbsp (20 g) chia seeds

For the crusts, preheat the oven to 350°F (175°C, gas mark 4), and grease a 12-cup mini muffin pan.

Place the dates and raisins in a bowl, cover them with ⅓ cup (80 ml) of the hot water and let them stand for 10 minutes.

To make the tart crusts, pulse the oats in a food processor for a minute or so, until they resemble coarse oat flour. Transfer them to a mixing bowl, and stir in the cinnamon and vanilla bean paste.

Put the butter and remaining ⅓ cup (80 ml) of water in a separate bowl, and stir until the butter is melted.

Drain the dates and raisins, leaving them wet. In a blender, blend them until they are smooth, then add them to the oatmeal mixture. Stir in the butter mixture and mix the ingredients until combined. Roll the mixture into one clump; it should feel a little crumbly but still hold together. Wrap the dough in plastic wrap and refrigerate it for 15 minutes.

Clean a work surface, then dust it with the buckwheat flour. With a rolling pin, roll out the dough so it's approximately 1⁄16 inch (2 mm) thick. Use a 3-inch (8-cm) cookie cutter to cut out twelve disks. Using a spatula, transfer each tart crust to a cup of the prepared pan. Bake the crusts for 20 minutes, or until they are golden and firm to the touch.

While the tart crusts bake, make the jam. In a small saucepan, cook the blackberries and cherry juice over medium heat. Gently break the berries down with a spoon as they cook. When the juices start releasing, which should only take a minute or two, add the chia seeds, and reduce the heat to low. The mixture should become more jamlike in texture after 5 minutes. Remove it from the heat if it gets too thick, as you need to be able to spoon it into the crusts.

Remove the crusts from the oven, and allow them to cool a little. Spoon the jam into the crusts. Let the tarts set for 15 minutes, and serve them when ready to eat.

MINT CHOCOLATE MOUSSE

This is such a lovely dessert, and so simple to make. It's high in magnesium and rich in nutrients. The mint cuts through and flavors wonderfully, and the avocado creates a silky creaminess, while adding an extra hit of goodness. This recipe shows that, by using complementary flavor profiles, you can enjoy desserts without them having to be overly sweet.

Serves 2

¼ cup (24 g) very finely chopped fresh mint leaves, plus a few whole mint leaves for garnish

1 avocado, halved

1¾ cups (420 ml) coconut cream

1¼ cups (200 g) pitted dried Medjool dates

½ cup (50 g) unsweetened cocoa powder

3 tbsp (45 ml) melted coconut oil

1 tbsp (15 g) vanilla bean paste

In a food processor, process the mint, avocado, coconut cream, dates, cocoa powder, coconut oil and vanilla bean paste until the mixture is completely smooth.

Pour the mousse into four 6-oz (180-ml) ramekins, and refrigerate them for 1 hour to set the mousse. Garnish the mousse with the reserved mint leaves and serve.

Acknowledgments

Thank you to my editor Jenna and my publisher Will at Page Street Publishing, and thanks also to my copyeditor Dianne and to Rosie and Meg.

Huge love and thanks to Mike and Ruby (Ziggy too), the loves of my life, whose days are frequently disrupted by my notions to whip up a new recipe and live with the mess and the constant works-in-progress. My mum, for her unwavering belief, support and inspiration. My siblings: Erin, for the patience, constant support, humoring me and honest advice (and for helping with food prep!); Martin, for showing me backbone, kindness and unparalleled entertainment; and Patsy, for our adventures, your knowledge of herbs and setting me on this holistic journey to health. My dad, for his humor and encouragement.

Michelle, for our friendship, the chats, guidance and for being my touchstone. Sinead, for your loveliness and for supporting Make Me Sugar Free from the very beginning.

Vanessa, for the incredible friendship, for never judging, getting on board with all my notions and for being my home away from home. Lisa, for your intuition in saying what I needed to hear when I needed it most.

My (breakfast club) Wingmen: Adam, for always having my back, and Gribby, for the foot stomps and the laughs.

To all the chief tasters, especially Niamh, Bernie, Angela, Lauren, Leah and Meabh.

Enormous thanks to my gorgeous, talented clients, who have actively supported and helped me grow the Make Me Sugar Free community: Ferne, Vas, Tanya, Mario, Luke, Jody, Natasha, Rosie and Amber.

Thanks also to Henry, Rosie, Conor, Julia, Grace, Biddy, Ellis, Chris, Meabh, Sean, Deb, Andy, Florrie, Spencer, Ant (Bolly), Daniel, Tommy, Maura, Martin, Maureen, Paddy, Caroline, Eileen, Nikki, Gavin, MJ, Simone, Christine, Yvonne, Ian, Anna, Lynette, Dr. Kanayama, Tanya, Sheila, Nicholas, Ryan, Tahir, Wim, Tom for legal, Paddy for PR and to every one of you who in some way has lent your support, from liking my recipe posts to spreading the word, and to the Make Me Sugar Free Instagram community, whose feedback means the world.

About the Author

Leisa is a qualified nutrition and health coach and is the founder of www.makemesugarfree.com. Cooking for family and friends has always been a passion of hers, especially the alchemy of transforming basic ingredients into something divinely nourishing, fortifying and delicious.

After suffering from years of endometriosis, Leisa decided against the hysterectomy that was being proposed as the last medical option. Instead, she chose a noninvasive, nutritional and holistic approach to healing, which was the catalyst for her sugar-free lifestyle and, ultimately, her continued health. Leisa shares her sugar-free recipes and experiences on her blog and on Instagram @makemesugarfree.

She lives in the country in County Mayo, Ireland, with her husband, daughter, dog and two cats.

Index